Taming Microaggressions

A Framework for Enhancing Teaching and Learning

Sylvester Ngoma, PhD

Dedication

To Dr. Chester M. Pierce, the psychiatrist who coined the term *microaggression.*

PUBLISHER

Berking Publishing House

North Carolina, USA.

Table of Contents

Acknowledgments

I want to thank everyone who made this book possible, particularly the teachers and students who allowed me to complete the research on microaggressions.

Introduction

A growing number of voices have been expressing disenchantment with the current state of public education in the United States, especially in the aftermath of the COVID-19 pandemic. The need to improve student learning and enhance the quality of instruction is ubiquitous in recent educational research literature and trade publications. There seems to be widespread agreement that K-12 education is in dire need of reforms despite some noticeable strides over the years.

Rethinking and reimagining this sector, which is so paramount to the fabric of this country, entails a critical appraisal of current educational practices and the traditional framework from which teaching and learning were conceptualized. This book offers unique insights grounded in educational practices from insiders' perspectives. It is organized into three main sections. The first section, "Enhancing the Quality of Career and Technical Education by Minimizing the Interference of Microaggressions," presents the findings of a qualitative study based on grounded theory on a framework to minimize the interference of microaggressions in Career and Technical Education (CTE) classes" It suggests a framework for taming microaggressions through education and deterrence. Section 1 comprises three chapters: Microaggressions Background and Scope, Microaggressions Management Framework, and Empowerment Framework.

Section 2, "Fueling Organizational Performance and Instructional Effectiveness," addresses different types of leadership and suggests an effective blend of school leadership that can unlock the intellectual capital of students and teachers. It has three chapters: A Blended Model of Educational Leadership, Drawing From Other Types of Leadership, and Improving Instruction Quality and Managing Diversity.

The third section, "Bolstering Teachers' Professional Identity: A Look at Compensation Plans," examines the perils of current teacher compensation systems along with the teacher workload. It questions the essence of pay-for-performance plans and advocates for a raise in teacher pay levels. It has two chapters: A Critical Appraisal of Teacher Remuneration and The Paradox of Teacher Performance Operationalization.

The book is intended to shed further light on what really goes on in the classroom from educators' and students' perspectives. I was bolstered in this endeavor by the responses I received from colleagues, students, parents, and friends whenever I shared some of my views on American education. Several of them enriched the discussion with their own ideas and extrapolations. They helped shape the final draft of this book. I am approaching the notion of education with a frame of reference. I have a mix of college and high school teaching experience, having taught in Vermont, North Carolina, California, and overseas. From an immigrant's perspective, I live the paradox and agony of the U.S. education system with amazement and dismay. Unless decision makers approach K-12 education differently, educational excellence will continue to be an elusive and enigmatic dream. This is a tale of education in black and white.

SECTION 1

Enhancing the Quality of Career and Technical Education by Minimizing the Interference of Microaggressions

Chapter 1

Microaggressions Background and Scope

Abstract

Over the last 4 decades, studies have substantiated the adverse, long-lasting impact of microaggressions in education. CTE programs are not immune from the devastating effects of the subtle and covert nature of microaggressions. This study presents a framework for boosting the quality of CTE instruction by minimizing instances of microaggressions. Through open coding, selective coding, and axial data coding, this grounded theory study involving 56 students and 12 teachers highlights two critical success factors: (a) psychological safety and student engagement congruence and (b) student empowerment and microaggression deterrence congruence. The main finding is that student empowerment through microaggressions management tactics along with enhanced organizational culture is positively associated with improved efficacy, whereas permissive CTE settings exert negative influence, leading to more devastating effects than initially assumed. A conceptual framework to reduce the interference of microaggressions with the goal of enhancing the quality of CTE instruction is proposed. Implications for practice are also discussed.

Introduction

It has emerged from extant research that student participation in science, technology, engineering, and math (STEM) fields encompassing CTE programs has grown exponentially over the years (Anderson, 2009). With regard to CTE programs specifically, it has been reported that 77% of ninth-grade public school students enrolled in 2009 participated in CTE by their senior year in 2013 (Ashford, 2020). Moreover, almost 98% of U.S. high schools offer some form of CTE programs, including coursework, work-based learning (such as on-the-job training, internships, practicums, clinical experiences, or cooperative education), and career pathways (U.S. Department of Education [USDE], 2019). Enrollment in CTE programs has been associated with positive outcomes, including increased graduation rates (Castellano et al., 2014), credits accumulation, and successful college mathematics experience (Neild et al., 2015). In 2018, the CTE concentrator graduation rate in North Carolina CTE programs was 99.2%, according to the North Carolina Department of Public Instruction (2023).

Despite their popularity and relative success, however, these programs still face a cohort of challenges, such as low levels of female participation; funding and staff capacity; negative perceptions of CTE; lack of transportation for work-based learning; language barriers; lack of support services; inflexible scheduling; recruitment and retention of qualified, diverse teachers; program screening criteria; limited long-term outcome data; limited information on evidence-based strategies (Government Accountability Office, 2022); and stereotype threat (Heilman, 2001).

In addition to these challenges, the prevalence of discipline-related incidents spurred by prejudice or bias in U.S. schools is on the rise. It was reported that more than one out of five students experience bullying, and one out of five students is chronically absent, with 7 million students missing 15 or more days of school in 2015–2016 (USDE, 2019). A study reported 7,103 single-bias incidents involving 8,552 victims, of which 57.6% were motivated by race, ethnicity, ancestry, or bias; 20.1% by religion; 2.7% by gender identity; 2.0% by disability; 16.7% by sexual orientation; and 0.9% by gender (U.S. Department of Justice, 2019). Moreover, the COVID-19 pandemic had a significant impact on the education sector.

In the post-COVID pandemic era, several incidents of discipline problems and altercations have been reported in schools. According to the 2021 *Report on Indicators of School Crime and Safety*, public schools reported 1.4 million incidents of crime during the 2019–2020 school year, an increase in cyberbullying compared to 2009–2010 (16% vs. 8%), an increase in student verbal abuse of teachers (10% vs. 5%), an increase in student acts of disrespect for teachers (15% vs. 9%), and widespread disorder in the classroom (4% vs. 3%; Irwin et al., 2021). Another report, the 2023 *Report on the Condition of Education*, noted that in April 2022, roughly 70% of public schools saw an increase in the number of students seeking mental health services since the breakout of the Coronavirus Pandemic (Irwin et al., 2023). Research has shown that victims of bullying are susceptible to experiencing depression and anxiety, truancy, dropout, and health problems (Hornor, 2018; Swearer & Hymel, 2015). It is worth noting that dropout rates in American high schools remain high, especially for certain minority groups (American Indian, Hispanic, and Black).

A large and growing body of research has ascertained the pervasiveness of microaggressions and their adverse effects in educational environments (Berk, 2017a; Sue, Capodilupo, Torino, Bucceri, et al.,

2007; Williams, 2020). Extant literature has amply shown that microaggressions provide a backdrop for hostility, tension, and conflict (Williams, 2020). They can cause such severe effects as depression, anxiety, impostor syndrome, and burnout (Nadal, 2018; Nadal et al., 2021), negatively impacting productivity and self-efficiency (Cohen et al., 2009). Furthermore, they can engender self-doubt, stress, and tension. These emotions are known to be "silent killers of student engagement" (Brookfield, 2015, p. 76). Such an environment is known to contribute to psychologically unsafe working conditions (Edmondson, 2018). Left unaddressed or incorrectly approached, microaggressions can create hostile learning environments, adversely impacting the quality of instruction and creating learning barriers (Smith et al., 2007; Williams, 2020). Low retention, for example, can be linked to microaggressions (Williams, 2020).

In educational environments where microaggressions have free rein, the potential for interference in teaching-learning practices looms large. Microaggressions may adversely impact the ability of students to take risks, be candid, volunteer, participate in learning activities, support peers, and make mistakes. R. Brown (1990) noted that behaviors such as asking for help, admitting errors, and seeking feedback exemplify threats. Research has shown that the potential for threat, embarrassment, or public humiliation inhibits learning (Argyris, 1982).

Conversely, psychological safety appears to facilitate learning (Hirak et al., 2012), performance, and team efficacy (Edmondson, 1999). Extant research has established a positive congruence between psychological safety and success, innovation, and learning. Essentially, student engagement is a critical enabling driver of academic achievement, retention, and well-being (Thomas & Nair, 2023). Student engagement drives educational outcomes (Finn & Zimmer, 2012).

This qualitative research examines common microaggressions that interfere with the quality of CTE instruction and suggests a framework for creating a psychologically safe CTE environment that is conducive to high-quality, inclusive, and equitable CTE instruction. The purpose is to encourage humanistic practices that minimize microaggressions, improve teaching and learning, promote student engagement, and enhance the quality of CTE instruction. This research addresses the question, What critical factors can reduce the interference of microaggressions in CTE classes and influence the quality of CTE instruction? To answer this question, a qualitative study focused on grounded theory was employed to uncover those factors using open and axial coding techniques (Charmaz, 2006).

Statement of the Problem

Burgeoning scholarship supports the argument that microaggressions negatively affect educational practices (Berk, 2017c; J. Y. Kim & Meister, 2023; Williams, 2020). While they are micro, these aggressions have a macro impact that can silently snowball into major problems in educational settings. Microaggressions can impair student engagement, undermine teaching effectiveness, and impede learning and problem-solving, leading to underperformance, absenteeism, disengagement from learning, and mental or emotional withdrawal. In a nutshell, microaggressions can adversely affect mental health, create physical health problems, perpetuate stereotypes, increase stress and negative feelings, lower productivity, and generate a hostile climate (Okazaki, 2009; Sue, 2010b; Sue et al., 2019).

The hostile and invalidating climate can lead to anger, depression, stress, anxiety, loss of self-esteem, and even rage (Sue, 2010a). These effects can subsequently have long-lasting consequences on victims (O'Keefe & Wingate, 2013) because they are constant, cumulative, and energy-depleting, unlike regular daily incivilities

(Sue et al., 2019). In essence, microaggressions have been linked to disengagement, disidentification, burnout, turnover (J. Y. Kim & Meister, 2023; Meister et al., 2017), and psychological trauma (Auguste et al., 2021; Capodilupo et al., 2010; Dodge, 2019; Henfield, 2011; Moody & Lewis, 2019; Murray, 2020; Sue, Capodilupo, Torino, Bucceri, et al., 2007). Empirical evidence establishes a significant correlation between teacher stress and burnout with poor student outcomes (Herman et al., 2018).

Furthermore, numerous studies have underscored the strategic importance of a positive school climate in influencing learning outcomes. Specifically, research has substantially shown that a positive school climate that fosters a nurturing, safe, and supportive educational environment can enhance class attendance, academic achievement, and retention and graduation rates (Cohen et al., 2009). Subsequently, a positive classroom atmosphere is conducive to quality instruction and effective student learning. Conversely, microaggressions have negative bearings on student learning and classroom climate. Where they have free rein, students tend to underachieve and teachers tend to undermine their own teaching practices.

It has been argued that students who claim to be victims of microaggressions play the victim card and are just too weak to handle hurtful words (Barbash, 2015). Yet, as noted earlier, there is a considerable body of research on the harmful effects of microaggressions (Berk, 2017b; Sue, Capodilupo, Torino, Bucceri, et al., 2007). Given their harmful effects and the toxic climate they engender, microaggressions can negatively and significantly affect different functional aspects of student performance (Keith, 2016). They can lead to underachievement, absenteeism or truancy, dropout, assault, and bullying (Gottfredson & Gottfredson, 2001). These can be attributable to a congruence of other factors, including (but not limited to) negative school climate, insufficient instructional support, socioeconomic conditions, lack of parental involvement, and personal responsibility. Thus, minimizing causal factors of student disengagement in the classroom by creating a positive and supportive learning environment can play a significant role in the prevention and reduction of student dropout rates, absenteeism cases, and classroom tensions.

Research suggests that an educational component is the centerpiece for reducing bullying and microaggressions. A study by McCallion and Feder (2013) found that school-based bullying prevention programs produced positive results by reducing bullying and cyberbullying by up to 25%. Williams et al. (2020) reported that the Racial Harmony Workshop, an initiative based on functional analytic psychotherapy and acceptance and commitment therapy aimed at reducing racial bias and microaggressions, resulted in improved mood and increased positive feelings toward a marginalized group.

Learning is an exploratory and dynamic process that encompasses social interaction, decision-making, hypothesis-making and testing, and affective and emotional investment. Essentially, learning is the raison d'être of all teaching. Teaching is undertaken for learning to occur. The success of any teaching can, therefore, best be judged in terms of the learning that results from it. Thus, an educational environment devoid of microaggressions is best suited for full engagement, active learning, and academic success.

Student performance may suffer in a classroom environment fraught with mistrust, tension, and hostility. It is hard for students to thrive academically if their ideas, cultural values, experiences, aspirations, and actions are dismissed, ridiculed, or demeaned. Anxiety, fear of ridicule or public humiliation, and self-doubt can set in, leading to what Brookfield (2006) termed "pedagogical hypertension" (p. 76). Ultimately, this may result in disengagement from learning or blockage of learning. Externally, students may appear to be serene while experiencing learning-threatening emotions internally. Heightened tension in the classroom can only undermine the student's ability to learn freely and actively and the teacher's ability to teach effectively and efficiently.

Furthermore, the notion of confrontation is inherently ubiquitous in the argument culture and in the fabric of a classroom where sarcasm, personal attacks, criticisms, insults, arguments, and invalidations occur on a regular basis. Tannen (1998) proffered that the argument culture can contribute to "alienating, separating, and disconnecting people" (p. 25). Fundamentally, such an adversarial environment can be an ideal ground for culture confrontation, race confrontation, prejudice confrontation, social status confrontation, social affiliation confrontation, gender confrontation, sexual orientation confrontation, and religious affiliation confrontation. Unless there is adequate psychological and pedagogical preparation of educators and students, a classroom where microaggressions predominate can easily turn into unmanageable chaos, which will ultimately and negatively affect the learning process.

Conceptual Background

Over 5 decades ago, Dr. Chester M. Pierce (1970), a Harvard University psychiatrist who was then-chairman of Black Psychiatrists of America, coined the term *microaggression* to encapsulate a myriad of "offensive mechanisms" (p. 472) used against Black people in the United States to psychologically coerce them into accepting the disenfranchised state they were in. Sue, Capodilupo, Torino, and Bucceri (2007) described those racial microaggressions as "brief, everyday exchanges that send denigrating messages to people of color because they belong to a racial minority group" (p. 273). The term *microaggression* has since expanded to include various marginalized groups such as specific racial/ethnic, gender, nationality, religious, socioeconomic status, and sexual orientation groups (Berk, 2017c). Microaggressions stem from a host of internal and external factors, such as prejudicial beliefs and attitudes, implicit bias (Sue et al., 2019), learned behaviors, and aversive racism (Williams, 2020). Due to their subtle or covert nature, microaggressions can be hard to detect yet can have psychologically devastating effects on victims. They are capable of destroying peace and group harmony as well as the morale of the individual and team (Desai et al., 2023). *Microinequity* is another word for *microaggression* in the business world.

Conceptually, the term *microaggression* has also evolved from subtle "putdowns" (Pierce et al., 1977, p. 66) of Blacks to hostile behaviors and indignities directed toward different marginalized or targeted groups (Nadal et al., 2014; Sue, 2010a). Sue, Capodilupo, Torino, and Bucceri's (2007) definition provides a practical, semantic delineation of the contours of this term as it is used today: "Brief and commonplace daily verbal, behavioral, and environmental indignities, whether intentional or unintentional, which communicate hostile, derogatory, or negative slights, invalidations, and insults to an individual or group because of their marginalized status in society" (p. 271). Williams (2020) postulated that microaggressions are "learned behaviors, taught through observational learning and other social mechanisms from an early age" (p. 35).

Examples of microaggressions abound. They include presumed incompetence, abrupt and rude interruptions, explaining for others (aka "mansplaining" or "womansplaining"), insensitive remarks, devaluing others' contributions (Berk, 2017b, 2017c), ascription of intelligence, assumption of criminal status, myth of meritocracy, pathologizing of cultural values, second-class citizen treatment, being invisible due to race, environmental omissions, being low achieving, and being alien in one's own land (Sue, Capodilupo, Torino, Bucceri, et al., 2007). Regarding the classifications of microaggressions, Sue,

Capodilupo, Torino, and Bucceri (2007) identified three broad categories: microassaults, microinsults, and microinvalidations. Microassaults are verbal or nonverbal discriminatory actions or attacks that convey a hurtful message. Microinsults are intentional or unintentional, verbal or nonverbal, conscious or unconscious, subtle or covert snubs, putdowns, or sarcastic remarks intended to demean the victim (Berk, 2017a). Microinvalidations are described as communications that "exclude, negate, or nullify the psychological thoughts, feelings, or experiential reality of the victim" (Berk, 2017c, p. 67).

Research Methodology

Research Design

This study adopts a grounded theory approach to attempt to uncover and understand the elusive social phenomenon being investigated. Strauss and Corbin's (1990, 1998) systematic procedures were selected for the elucidation of microaggressions; the collection of reliable data from educators and learners; and an in-depth interpretation of events, happenings, and instances of microaggressions. This approach allows researchers to transcend and supersede their own theoretical ideas, beliefs, feelings, and perceptions in order for new insights to emerge (Creswell, 2007).

Throughout the years, several instruments have been utilized to attempt to uncover patterns, perceptions, and experiences of microaggressions as well as personal motives that drive them. Some of the commonly utilized instruments include the Positive and Negative Affectivity Schedule (Watson et al., 1988), Multidimensional Scale of Perceived Discrimination (Molero et al., 2013), Implicit Association Test (Greenwald et al., 1998), LGBT People of Color Microaggressions Scale (Balsam et al., 2011), Racial and Ethnic

Microaggressions Scale (Nadal, 2011), Ethnic Microaggressions Scale (Huynh, 2012), Racial Microaggressions Scale (Torres-Harding et al., 2012), Homonegative Microaggressions Scale (Wright & Wegner, 2012), Gendered Microaggression Inventory (Yang & Carroll, 2016), Student Microaggression Inventory (Berk, 2017a), Cultural Cognitions and Actions Scale (Michaels et al., 2018), Overt-Covert Aggression Inventory (Miyazaki et al., 2003), and Gendered Racial Microaggressions Scale for Asian American Women (Keum et al., 2018). The list is not exhaustive.

In addition to quantitative instruments, numerous qualitative studies based on common qualitative approaches—case study, grounded theory, ethnography, phenomenology, and narrative—have amply heightened understandings of microaggressions experienced by marginalized groups with varying degrees of interpretive infallibility (Berk, 2017c; Gonzales et al., 2015; Hill et al., 1997; Solórzano et al., 2000; Sue, Capodilupo, Torino, Bucceri, et al., 2007; Thomas & Harden, 2008; Yosso et al., 2009). Several extant qualitative studies rely on self-reports (Gutiérrez y Muhs et al., 2012), recall (Wong et al., 2014), thematic synthesis (Thomas & Harden, 2008), thematic analysis (Braun & Clarke, 2006), and consensual qualitative research (Hill et al., 1997), with a multitude of data sources encompassing documents, observations, interviews, and audiovisual materials (Creswell, 2007).

The adopted grounded theory approach aims to explore the occurrences of microaggressions, causal conditions, context, actions taken in response, intervening conditions, and consequences in a CTE classroom environment. An electronic survey with a series of open-ended questions was sent to the study participants. Observation field notes, survey responses, and discussion notes were triangulated to construct a conceptual framework for CTE instruction quality enhancement.

Sample and Data Collection

The target population for this grounded theory study was full-time CTE teachers and students enrolled in CTE courses from Charlotte-Mecklenburg Schools (CMS). Using theoretical sampling methodology (Glaser & Strauss, 1967), a sample of 56 students and 12 teachers was drawn from this population. It was stratified into two sets of contributors—students and teachers—to gain a more in-depth and comprehensive understanding of the phenomenon. The sample was drawn from three of 34 high schools.

CMS offers over 20 CTE career pathways for high schools, including advanced manufacturing and engineering, architecture and engineering, automotive, biomedical science, business management, carpentry, cosmetology, culinary arts and hospitality, customer relationship management, digital marketing, energy and power, financial planning, game art design, graphic and digital design, interior design, nursing fundamentals, public safety, public safety—emergency management, public safety—firefighter technology, public safety—law enforcement and protection, software development, and sports and event marketing. A few faculty members from school districts outside of CMS were interested in the study. However, it was deemed necessary to limit the sample to CTE students and teachers within CMS with a diversity of attributes and characteristics to ensure the validity and transferability of the findings.

Research participants were asked to explain their perceptions of the nature of microaggressions they experienced or witnessed, the responses to microaggressions, the consequences of those microaggressions, the context of the microaggressions, the intervening conditions, and the interventions. Overall, this grounded theory study focused on the interpretation of the apparent connection between a microaggressive classroom environment and the subsequent quality (or lack thereof) of CTE instruction. Questions were designed to allow study participants to genuinely share their experiences. Academic discussions about the topic with several students and teachers over the past 5 years have provided an impetus and a foundation to pursue this research.

Following theoretical sampling and the generation of grounded theory by Strauss and Corbin (1998), three coding systems—open coding, axial coding, and selective coding—were used to allow me to find recurring themes that were important to respondents. The survey questions and academic discussions were designed to be comprehensive in scope. The results of the survey would elucidate my understanding of microaggressions in an attempt to help improve the learning and teaching processes by minimizing their interference in CTE. During the discussion phase, several students reported knowing about microaggressions but not knowing the phraseology to describe the phenomenon. Some indicated being surprised that the topic of microaggressions had received inadequate attention in schools despite their widely recognized and increasing impact on students' mental health and performance.

Study 1: Students

The primary goal of Study 1 was to develop an understanding of microaggressions faced by students and how they impacted their learning. It was designed for students to share their insights into their perceptions of microaggression realities in the classroom. For Study 1, data were obtained from 56 students who completed a survey electronically. This was followed by face-to-face academic discussions to elicit students' written responses. Questions were organized into four sections: perception of personal ability, perception of personal contribution, race and gender stereotyping, and cultural values.

Students were predominantly African American (23, or 41.1%), Hispanic (20, or 35.7%), Asian (8, or 14.3%), White (3, or 5.4%), and Other (2, or 3.6%). Their ages were 14 (10.9%), 15 (34.5%), 16 (25.5%), 17 (18.2%), and 18 or older (10.9%). They were all enrolled as full-time students at different grade levels in four CMS schools: 9th grade (44.6%), 10th grade (28.6%), 11th grade (16.1%), and 12th grade (10.7%). More than half (58.2%) were males, 38.2% were female, and 3.6% chose not to reveal their gender. The majority of students took one CTE course (46.3%), 25.9% took two CTE courses, 13% took three CTE courses, 11.1% took four CTE courses, and 5% did not specify the number of CTE courses they took. Students were selected if they met the following requirements: (a) enrolled as a full-time student in CMS, (b) taking at least one CTE course, (c) experienced or observed instances of microaggressions, and (d) ability to communicate in English.

A 31-item, anonymous survey was administered to CTE students in a 2-week time frame in May 2023 to solicit their views on microaggressions they may have experienced or witnessed. The questions were designed to cover four aspects of microaggressions: perception of personal ability, perception of personal contribution, race and gender stereotyping, and cultural values and communication styles. With respect to student survey questions, six were designed to capture perceptions of personal abilities, six for perceptions of personal contribution, five for perceptions of race and gender stereotyping, and six for cultural values and communication styles. Overall, 23 questions made up the student survey, in addition to eight questions about demographic data.

The diversity of the student population allowed me to address the survey questions and collect a wide range of responses from students of different backgrounds. To get students to participate willingly in the study, I promised that their responses would remain confidential and that there would be no attempt to identify any individual participant. Overall, 56 students completed the survey. All of these students were enrolled in CTE courses. Their demographic diversity was representative of the target population, as can be seen in Table 1, which summarizes the students' demographic characteristics.

Table 1. Summary of Students' Demographics

Demographic Category	Number	Percentage
Age		
14	6	10.9
15	19	34.5
16	14	25.5
17	10	18.2
18 or older	6	10.9
Grade Level	25	44.6
9th grade		
10th grade	16	28.6
11th grade	9	16.1
12th grade	6	10.7
Gender	32	58.2
Male		
Female	21	38.2
Prefer not to say	2	3.6
Ethnicity		
Asian	8	14.3
African American	23	41.1
Hispanic	20	35.7
White	3	5.4
Native American	0	0.0
Other	2	3.6
Years Taking CTE Courses		
1	30	56.6
2	10	18.9
3	7	13.2
4	4	7.5
5 or more	2	3.8

Demographic Category	Number	Percentage
CTE Course Taken		
Agricultural Education	1	1.8
Business, Finance, and Information Technology Education	14	25.5
Technology Engineering and Design Education	11	20.0
Trade and Industrial Education	4	7.3
Other	25	45.5
Number of CTE Courses Taken		
1	25	46.3
2	14	25.9
3	7	13.0
4	6	11.1
5 or more	2	3.7

Study 2: Teachers

Study 1 was complemented by Study 2, which was designed to gain insights into teachers' perceptions of this social phenomenon within the CTE environment. Both studies were conducted almost concurrently. For Study 2, teachers' questions addressed four areas: perception of expertise or competence, perception of performance, race and cultural stereotyping, and cultural values and communication styles. Teachers were randomly selected based on the following criteria: (a) employed as a full-time teacher in the CTE department in a CMS school, (b) teaching at least one CTE course, and (c) experienced or observed instances of microaggressions.

All of the teachers were employed full-time. Teachers were predominantly African American (7, or 58.3%), White (2, or 16.7%),

Asian (1, or 8.3%), and Other (2, or 16.7%). Teachers' ages ranged from 20–29 (8.3%), 30–39 (16.7%), 40–49 (33.3%), and 50 and up (41.7%). With regard to their education levels, the majority (83.3%) had master's degrees, 8.3% had undergraduate degrees, and 8.3% had doctorate degrees or had taken postgraduate courses. Two-thirds (66.7%) taught business, finance, and information technology courses; 16.7% taught technology engineering and design education courses; and 16.7% taught other courses. There were more females (75%) than males (25%). With regard to the number of students taught, 16.7% taught 1–19 students, 8.3% taught 20–39 students, 16.7% taught 40–59 students, 16.7% taught 60–79 students, and 41.7% taught 80 or more students. These teachers had several years of experience teaching CTE courses: 33.3% had 0–5 years, 41.7% had 6–11 years, 8.3% had 12–17 years, and 16.7% had 18–23 years of experience in CMS.

A 36-item, anonymous survey was administered to CTE teachers to solicit their views on microaggressions, perceived or real, in CTE classes. Teachers' questions addressed four areas: perception of expertise or competence, perception of performance, race and cultural stereotyping, and cultural values and communication styles. With respect to teachers' survey questions, five were meant to gauge perceptions of their expertise or competence, seven for perceptions of their performance, six for perceptions of race and gender stereotyping, and four for cultural values and communication styles. Overall, 22 questions made up the teacher survey, in addition to 14 questions about demographic data.

CTE teachers who participated in the study were willing participants. They were distributed over three CMS schools. The survey was sent to over 30 CTE teachers. Overall, 12 teachers completed the survey electronically. Most of them also shared additional thoughts through further face-to-face discussions. Their contributions were paramount to uncover additional insights into microaggressions in CTE classes from their perspective. Table 2 summarizes the teachers' demographic characteristics.

Table 2. Summary of Teachers' Demographics

Demographic Category	Number	Percentage
Age		
20–29	1	8.3
30–39	2	16.7
40–49	4	33.3
50 or older	5	41.7
Education		
Associate's	0	0.0
Undergraduate	1	8.3
Graduate	10	83.3
Doctorate/postgraduate	1	8.3
Gender		
Male	3	25
Female	9	75
Prefer not to say	0	0.0
Employment Status		
Full-time	12	100.0
Part-time	0	0.0
Ethnicity		
Asian	1	8.3
African American	7	58.3
Hispanic	0	0.0
White	2	16.7
Native American	0	0.0
Other	2	16.7

Demographic Category	Number	Percentage
Years Teaching CTE Courses		
0–5	4	33.3
6–11	5	41.7
12–17	1	8.3
18–23	2	16.7
24–29	0	0.0
30 or more	0	0.0
Number of Students		
1–19	2	16.7
20–39	1	8.3
40–59	2	16.7
60–79	2	16.7
80 or more	5	41.7
CTE Courses Taught		
Business, Finance, and Information Technology Education	8	66.7
Technology Engineering and Design Education	2	16.7
Trade and Industrial Education	0	0.0
Agricultural Education	0	0.0
Other	2	16.7

Data Analysis

While open coding and selective coding allowed for the naming, identification, and categorization of microaggressions, axial coding allowed me to connect the categories and sort out relationships between them. The triangulation of observation field notes, survey responses, and discussion notes aided in minimizing and suspending subjective, preconceived ideas or biases and optimizing accuracy in data collection and inferences (Johnson et al., 2020). It also helped ensure methodological rigor. Chapter 2 presents the results of this grounded theory analysis and suggests a framework for managing microaggressions.

Chapter 2

Microaggressions Management Framework

A Conceptual Model for Microaggressions Management

This grounded theory investigation proposes a theoretical model for coping with microaggressions and improving learning and teaching experiences, presented in Figure 1. It schematizes links between causal conditions, context, intervening conditions, management strategies, and consequences of microaggressions.

Figure 1. Model of Microaggression Management Strategy

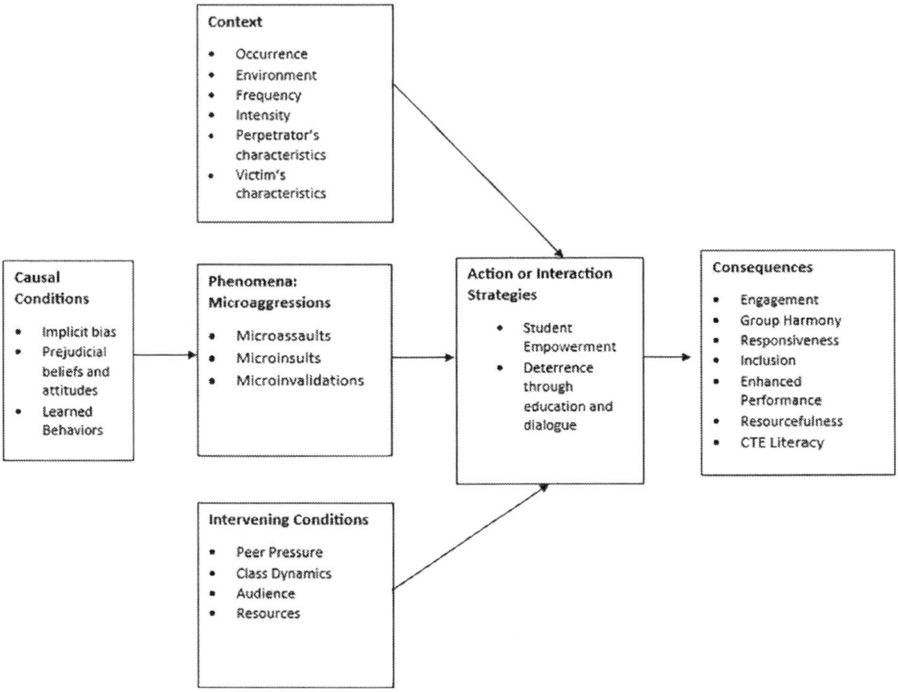

Causal Conditions

Three distinct types of causal conditions of microaggressions emerged from the data: (a) implicit bias, (b) prejudicial beliefs and attitudes (Sue et al., 2019), and (c) learned behaviors (Williams, 2020). Berk (2017c) defined *microaggressions* as "*explicit* expressions of bias and attitudes and blatant acts of prejudice" (p. 99). It is worth noting that implicit bias or unconscious bias, which can occur without recognition (Banaji & Greenwald, 2013), differs from deliberate prejudices (or explicit bias). The following statements from some study participants reflect social stereotypes based on intentional or unintentional slants. They are highly loaded with metamessages.

Students' quotes:

One student was quoted as telling another student, "This book is not for you. Africans can't read. You don't even have libraries in Africa."

As he was leaving his seat, a student was warned, "Don't leave your schoolbag here. You know he is from Puerto Rico. Puerto Ricans will steal anything."

Student to another student: "You have slave feet! I am sure you can run fast."

A White student started a response to his Black teacher this way: "Listen, boy."

Similarly, teachers also must examine their own biases, such as halo effect, gender bias, racial/ethnic bias, sexual orientation bias, and incompetence bias. Students reported cases of some teachers who underestimated their students' cognitive abilities; teachers whose impressions of students affected their rapport with those students (halo effect); teachers who questioned their students' intelligence; and teachers who judged their students based on race, religion, or sexual orientation. The following biased statements from teachers tend to undercut and, indeed, undermine teacher effectiveness.

Teachers' quotes:

One teacher described his students in this manner: "These students are thugs, man. They like to fight."

Teacher: "My students can't read. I wonder how they [administration] have been promoting them [students]. How do they expect me to teach them?"

Teacher: "When children have children, this is the result. Students don't know how to act, and parents can't help."

This is what one teacher thought of her students' names: "Many of my students have ghetto names; you know they are coming from the 'hood.'"

Teacher: "Our students can read but don't read."

"No incorrect grammar is allowed in my classroom."

It is hard to pinpoint the underlying motives behind the natural inclinations that led to these statements. These feelings may have stemmed from bigotry, prejudice, bias, or discrimination. They could have been motivated by preferences associated with gender, ethnicity, socioeconomic status, religion, or other group-defining characteristics. They could also have been mere expressions of internalized behaviors resulting from socialization practices or prevailing cultural norms. Williams (2020) argued that racism is another factor besides the three causal factors cited earlier. *Aversive racism*, as she referred to it, is different from blatant, old-fashioned racism in that "aversive racists outwardly endorse fair and just treatment of all groups yet harbor feelings of discomfort toward people of color that may be unconscious" (Williams, 2020, p. 38).

Teachers must be adequately equipped and prepared to explore their own biases and blind spots. They must be trained to gain self-awareness and to challenge their own stereotypes and prejudices. Students and teachers must be armed with a toolbox of skills to manage stress, anxiety, and microaggressions. Teachers must adopt asset-based approaches, not deficit-based approaches, to teaching. It is their pedagogical duty to lead students to reexamine and challenge their preconceptions, attitudes, beliefs, prejudices, and biases. Many teachers are reluctant to talk about their own biases. The debate is not settled because of the fear of tackling and addressing one's conscious or unconscious internal biases. Silence is not the solution. Teachers must be brave enough to confront this topic because microaggressions can have harmful, long-term effects on students.

To succeed in achieving the intent of Perkins IV, the main support of CTE programs is "to improve the achievement of CTE students in relation to state academic standards and to ease their transition to postsecondary education" (Castellano et al., 2014, p. xv), it is important to minimize the influence of these causal conditions in CTE settings. Considering the countless and deleterious consequences of microaggressions—such as student disengagement, teachers' underperformance, students' underachievement, absenteeism, teacher turnover, and student dropout—in CTE programs, heightening teachers' and students' informed awareness of their own biases and prejudices can be an effective self-management tactic.

Context

Microaggressions do not occur in a vacuum; context matters. Understanding the what, when, where, who, why, and how is crucial for students and teachers to develop educated awareness of the manifestation, causal conditions, intervening conditions, interaction patterns, classroom dynamics (if it occurs in a classroom), impact on victims, audience, responses, and consequences of microaggressions. These contextual factors are paramount. The following questions should be addressed: What happened? Where did it happen? When did it happen? Why did it happen? Who was involved? How can it be prevented in the future? The teacher should allow an open dialogue around these questions with an attitude of neutrality. Figure 2 provides a schematic of a dialogue framework.

Figure 2. Microaggression Context Model

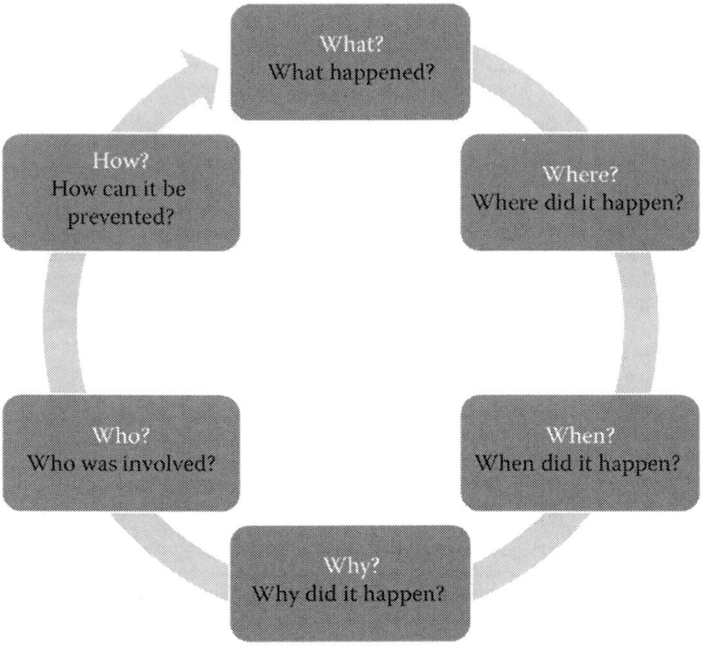

Microaggressions experienced in CTE environments vary in terms of frequency and intensity of the attacks. They also vary in terms of interaction patterns: student–to–student, student–to–teacher, teacher–to–student, and teacher–to–teacher. Learning about the occurrence, the environment where it occurs, the frequency of such incidents, the perpetrator's characteristics, the victim's characteristics, and the emotional states of individuals involved can provide insights into the underlying causes and proper coping strategies. It is important that learners take ownership of the learning and the learning environment. Teachers must set clear limits on what behavior is permissible in the classroom. Once norms, boundaries, and expectations are set, expectations are that fewer occurrences will take place, and optimal instruction can proceed with minimal disruptions.

It is worth noting that victims and perpetrators varied. The perpetrators were regular students and teachers who seemed to feel entitled to their behaviors. Some were unaware of the impact of their actions, which ranged from simple unintentional smears to extreme putdowns. The victims on the receiving end of microaggressions were a mixed group of individuals based on their learning disabilities, race/ethnicity, gender, nationality, religion, socioeconomic status, and sexual orientation. For them, the classroom does not provide much-needed safety, support, and protection, which creates various psychological effects. They can lose their self-confidence and self-esteem. Avoidance can be a response to a stressful situation (Woolfolk, 2004). Victims of classroom-related harassment are known to avoid the environment altogether.

Intervening Conditions Influencing Microaggressions

Several intervening conditions influence the what and the how of microaggressions. Notable among them are peer pressure, audience, classroom dynamics, and resources, which played a powerful role in occurrences and the responses to microaggressions. Peer pressure, particularly negative peer pressure, was uniquely influential because it promoted and encouraged conformity to unspoken group norms. Here are a few direct quotes by students that illustrate peer pressure:

> "You're going to let him talk to you like that?"
>
> "Don't let him get away with that!"
>
> "If that was me, man, we would be scrapping right now!"

These statements could instigate aggressive responses, and students often succumb to this type of peer pressure, forcing them to act or respond aggressively.

Having an audience affected students' responses to microaggressions. In some cases, it exacerbated peer pressure. Students' responses to microaggressions differed when there was an audience around. Fear of being ridiculed, reprimanded, or ostracized affected their responses. Some students tried hard not to appear weak, soft, helpless, or powerless around their peers. Some students appeared to be emotionally withdrawn, avoiding confrontation. It is essential that all students have a shared understanding of the expected classroom culture.

Classroom dynamics was another intervening condition that added another layer of complexity and sophistication to this phenomenon. Taken holistically, the dynamics of the classroom environment concerned classroom actors (students, teachers, teacher assistants, and administrators present in the classroom), their emotional states, behaviors, interactions, and learning and teaching processes. When students were immersed in learning, their productivity soared and incidents of microaggressions decreased. It is incumbent upon teachers to create a classroom culture that empowers students to work together.

Resources are fundamentally important assets for student success. If present, disparities and inequalities must be addressed promptly. Some students reported that they had a slow internet connection at home, lacked Wi-Fi at home, lost their Chromebooks, or did not have the required software. The lack of availability of resources affects students' behaviors. Lack of access to the same resources reinforces the notion of a "digital divide." This tends to push students to display disruptive behaviors. Equitable resources allow for the inclusion of all students. Given the diversity of CTE student populations, particularly in terms of race, ethnicity, gender, socioeconomic status, abilities, and learning disability status, it is imperative that all students have access to the same type of resources (hardware and software) and experience equitable and inclusive CTE instruction. School leadership must ensure that resources are accessible, relevant, and reflective of all students' identities, backgrounds, differences, and perspectives in CTE learning environments. This implies equitable allocation of resources and funding of programs. Students and teachers should be asked to contribute their input. Their input can guide the selection, adoption, and allocation of resources.

Microaggressions Typology

Through open and selective coding systems, 22 broad categories of microaggressions were chronicled:

1. Alien in one's own land,
2. Color-blindness,
3. Myth of meritocracy,
4. Ascription of intelligence,
5. Devaluation of technical competence,
6. Devaluation of physical presence,
7. Identity threat,
8. Pathologizing young woman's personal character,
9. Denial or ignorance of one's reality,
10. Exclusion,
11. Assumption of incompetence,
12. Name-calling,
13. Denial of individual racism,
14. Pathologizing of cultural values,
15. Assumption of criminal status,

16. Assumption of intellectual inferiority,
17. Offensive signs or pictures,
18. Sexist/heterosexist language,
19. Traditional gender-role prejudicing and stereotyping,
20. Degrading a racial or ethnic group,
21. Discomfort/disapproval of experience, and
22. Endorsing stereotypes.

Table 3 provides a thematic synthesis of microaggressions in CTE classrooms. Themes were adapted from Sue (2010b), Nadal et al. (2014), Berk (2017c), Barber et al. (2020), and J. Y. Kim and Meister (2023).

Table 3. Thematic Synthesis of Microaggressions in CTE Classrooms

Theme	Context	Microaggression Quote
Alien in one's own land	A student's response to the question, "Has anyone (a teacher or a classmate) ever devalued, invalidated, or diminished your contribution in a class activity?"	"A classmate once said that my opinions didn't matter in a group activity and called me a racial slur to back up the reason why my opinions didn't matter."
Color-blindness	A teacher reassigns a Hispanic student to a new seat because of disruptive behavior.	The student reacts angrily and says to another student: "This nigger keeps moving me, man! I swear to God! I am about to blank!" Shocked, the teacher asks, "Are you calling me the N-word?" Student: "You are a nigger, aren't you?" Then, quickly and unapologetically adds, "I call everybody nigger!" The teacher advises the student to refrain from using the N-word.

Theme	Context	Microaggression Quote
Devaluation of technical competence	Three quotes from three CTE teachers responding to the question, "Has anyone ever underestimated or overestimated your technical capabilities, your intelligence, or your competence?"	"Yes, someone once underestimated my technical abilities before. I just proved them wrong." (Teacher 1) "Yes. A colleague of mine, but she does not know that I know. I did not worry about it because karma is a gangster." (Teacher 2) "Yes. Sometimes people of other races automatically underestimate the value that a Black person may bring to the table." (Teacher 3)
Myth of meritocracy	A student expresses self-doubt.	"Sometimes I may know what they are talking about, but I always let some-one else respond because there are times when I doubt myself."
	A teacher confides to another teacher.	"My students can't read. I wonder how they [administration] have been promoting them [students]. How do they expect me to teach them?"
Ascription of intelligence	An African American student's response to the question, "Has anyone ever underes-timated or overesti-mated your personal capabilities, your intelligence, or your competence? Please explain."	"YES!!!!!!! I'm both overestimated in strength and underestimated in intelligence."
	An Asian student's response to the question, "Has anyone ever underestimated or overestimated your personal capabilities, your intelligence, or your competence?"	"They have overestimated my intelli-gence for years."

Theme	Context	Microaggression Quote
	A response to the question, "Has anyone ever underestimated or overestimated your personal contribution in a CTE class?"	"Yeah. Many people have overestimated my ability to understand and program a piece of code quickly."
	A Hispanic student's response to the question, "Has anyone ever underestimated or overestimated your personal capabilities, your intelligence, or your competence?"	"Yes, a lot of people think I'm dumb, mostly because I'm pretty quiet and because I'm a Latina. They also assume that I can't speak English."
	An African-American teacher's response to the question, "Has anyone (a teacher or a classmate) ever devalued, invalidated, dismissed, or diminished your performance in a class activity because of your race or your gender?"	"Yes. Sometimes people of other races automatically underestimate the value that a Black person may bring to the table."
Ascription of intelligence (*cont'd.*)	A teacher recalled torture from a former teacher when he was a student	"Yes, when I was in grade school. I had White teachers do this. I even had my second-grade teacher fired because of how she treated myself and other Black students. She basically tortured us. She was South African and this was in the early 80s."

Theme	Context	Microaggression Quote
Devaluation of physical presence	The presence of a student or teacher can be completely ignored. Students or teachers can also be constantly interrupted in formal discussions (Berk, 2017c; J. Y. Kim & Meister, 2023). Two students reported.	"The class was having a group discussion one day. Just before I spoke, the teacher said, 'You can say "pass" if you don't know.' He hurt my feelings by assuming that I did not know." "Yes. Sometimes people of other races automatically underestimate the value that a Black person may bring to the table."
Exclusion	Student excludes self from class participation.	"I have a hard time speaking up, and really just stick to doing my work without verbally participating in class as much as I can."
Identity threat	Two students talking about their CTE teachers.	"No one cares about anything he has to say." "When I first saw him, I thought he was stupid."
Denial or ignorance of one's reality	Regarding a Hispanic student who was born in the United States, one student says to another student:	"Can you ask him if he speaks English?"
Pathologizing dress code	A teacher was upset about a student's attire.	The teacher told the student, "I bet you be giving it up" (meaning she thinks the student is sexually active). The student concluded that the teacher called her a prostitute. She said, "This teacher basically called me a whore! I could not believe it!"
Assumption of incompetence	A student's response to the question, "Has anyone ever underestimated or overestimated your personal capabilities, your intelligence, or your competence?"	"Yes. A few days ago, we had a test in a CTE class. I was the first to finish, and almost everyone thought I cheated."

Theme	Context	Microaggression Quote
Name-calling	A teacher's response to the question, "Has anyone ever made implicitly or explicitly biased statements about you in CTE class based on your race, your ethnicity, or your gender? Please explain."	"Yes, I have been called the N-word in a student group chat at another school that was mostly White."
Denial of individual racism	A White student to a Black teacher.	Student: "Listen to me, boy!" Teacher: "Who are you calling 'boy'?" Student: "You. I call everybody 'boy.' I call my dad 'boy.'"
Pathologizing cultural values	An African-American student stunned his teacher with this strange inquiry	"I heard that Africans eat monkeys and have sex with them; that's how they catch Ebola. I saw it in a documentary. Is that true?"
Assumption of criminality	A student asks another student (who is half Arab, half Hispanic).	"Is your father Osama bin Laden? Are you a terrorist, too?"
	Staff member to teacher.	"These students are thugs, man. They like to fight."
	Student-to-student microaggression.	"Don't leave your schoolbag here. You know he is from Puerto Rico. Puerto Ricans will steal anything."
Assumption of intellectual inferiority	Teacher-to-student microaggression.	"One time, one of my teachers told the whole class (including me) that we were gonna fail. But we all passed."
	A student believes that a teacher treats students differently.	"I know a teacher who asks difficult questions to students of other races first before asking African American students. In that class, students of other races get more attention than African American students in some classes."

Theme	Context	Microaggression Quote
Offensive signs or pictures	A Hispanic student uses masking techniques to edit a picture of a monkey and replace the head of the monkey with a famous African-American movie star. The class is appalled when he asks.	"How do you like my design?"
Degrading a racial/ ethnic group	A teacher asks students about their most memorable moment at school as they are about to graduate. Before one Hispanic student has a chance to answer the question, another student interjects abruptly.	"The day he turned legal in the United States." The class bursts into laughter.
	A student jokingly tells a group of Hispanic students	"If Donald Trump is reelected, he is going to deport you, you, you, you, and you [pointing at individual students]. You're gonna be deported. There are too many illegal immigrants at this school."
Discomfort/ disapproval of experience	A White student uses a confederate flag as a course profile picture and as a background for each slide presentation.	"Nothing you will say will stop me from using this flag. I grew up loving it. You can't understand."

Theme	Context	Microaggression Quote
Denial of individual racism	A Hispanic male student is having a conversation with a female student close to the classroom door after the last bell, which signals the beginning of the class. The teacher comes out and asks the young man to enter the classroom.	Student complains, "This nigger is always in my shadow." Teacher asks, "Am I a nigger to you?" Student responds, "The word *nigger* means nothing to my generation. Your generation takes it too seriously."
Endorsing stereotypes	A student tells his classmate, a tall, athletic African-American student	"Why do you want to major in computer science? You are so big and tall; you should be a football player."
	A male student advises an African-American female student to drop a class	"Why are you taking Game Art and Design? Drop that class; it is for boys."
	A teacher asked students what they wanted to do after high school. One student answered for a Hispanic student.	"I know what you are going to do after you graduate! You are going to work in a construction job. That's what Mexicans do!"

The table encapsulates a sample of microaggressions that take place in CTE classrooms and on school grounds. There is not one form that is harmless. Communicated verbally and nonverbally, all these microaggressions can be powerful destroyers of student involvement, engagement, confidence, trust, and self-esteem, particularly for marginalized groups. They can, and indeed do, disincentivize course enrollment, involvement, and participation. In

STEM, where gender parity with regard to student enrollment is a major challenge, microaggressions such as assumption of inferiority or incompetence, devaluation of technical ability, degrading of physical presence, degrading of a racial or ethnic group, and pathologizing women's personal character only help reinforce the exclusion of female students from the programs, however appealing the programs can be.

Moreover, such microaggressions as stereotypical assumptions, invalidations of racial/cultural issues, overemphasis on weaknesses, and culturally insensitive remarks (Constantine & Sue, 2007) can lead to conflict, public humiliation, demoralization, shame, and embarrassment. There is experimental support for the notion that these interactions tend to be tense, raising anxiety levels, particularly for those with little or no prior exposure (Stephan & Stephan, 1985). Students who are constantly exposed to these stereotypical situations can feel nervous about the environment, which can inhibit their performance. The public shame, embarrassment, and humiliation microaggressions engender reinforce the feeling of impostorship (Brookfield, 2015). Hollingsworth et al. (2017) uncovered a correlation between some forms of racial microaggressions (namely, invisibility, low achievement or undesirable culture, and environmental invalidations) and suicidal ideation. The authors established the mediating role that depressive symptoms play between suicidal ideation and microaggressions.

Teachers also reported cases of devaluation of technical competence or physical presence, denial of one's reality, disapproval of experience, ascription of intelligence, and assumption of intellectual inferiority. A CTE teacher whose students produced exemplary programming work was asked in a virtual session: "Did you really teach them (students) that, or did they (students) learn on their own?" Research has established an association between underestimation of personal ability and greater stress levels (Torres et al.,

2010). As indicated earlier, these microaggressions can negatively affect teachers' efficiency and effectiveness, leading to burnout, retention problems, and attendance problems.

Consequences of Microaggressions

In essence, microaggressions can lead to withdrawal, disengagement, self-doubt, frustration, and anger. Insubordination, instructional unresponsiveness, and reduced motivation to participate in learning activities can, therefore, be by-products of these emotions. Students may demonstrate unpreparedness or unwillingness to learn or to participate in class activities. This can result in either resistance or blockage and cessation of learning. Students may disengage from the learning process, ostracize themselves, and become unresponsive or reactive. Their defensive and offensive impulses may be triggered. Their emotional states may affect their motivation and involvement in class activities. Their "socio-affective filter" (Stevick, 1976, p. 48) can be lowered or raised depending on negative or positive effects, leading to a set of challenges. There is extensive research on comprehensive input and socio-affective filters (Dulay et al., 1982; Krashen, 1982; Krashen & Terrell, 1983).

Wherever microaggressions are ubiquitous, teachers encounter discipline problems such as student insubordination, emotional detachment, mental withdrawal, unresponsiveness, seclusion, defeatism, disengagement, disidentification, animosity, and harassment. Williams (2020) summarized the harmful impact of microaggressions on victims' mental health. Those consequences include stress, depression, alcohol and substance abuse, posttraumatic stress disorder symptoms, suicide, anxiety, somatization, and obsessive-compulsive disorder.

One of the primary responsibilities of a teacher is to furnish a positive effect. This aids in driving high levels of student engagement for them to achieve academic success. It is quite unlikely that this goal can be achieved in a hostile educational environment where microaggressions are prevalent. Students can be unwilling to participate in class activities such as volunteering, taking risks, joining teams, asking questions, giving oral presentations, speaking up, expressing a viewpoint, and helping others. They may show some resistance toward proposed learning activities, agendas, teaching styles, communication styles, tests, and more. This resistance may affect their adherence to classroom activities. The consequences of microaggressions are severe if unaddressed, as can be seen in Figure 3.

When students are constantly subjected to microaggressions, they may struggle to complete learning activities effectively, attend classes consistently, or thrive in the classroom, resulting in reduced confidence. In addition to reduced confidence, microaggressions can also lead to reduced performance or self-efficacy, reduced motivation, decreased engagement, increased absenteeism, decreased morale, feeling of disconnectedness/decreased group harmony, and reduced satisfaction, as presented in Figure 3. It is worth pointing out that the impact of microaggressions is not always immediate or short-term. It can be mid-term or long-term.

Figure 3. Summary of Consequences of Microaggressions in CTE

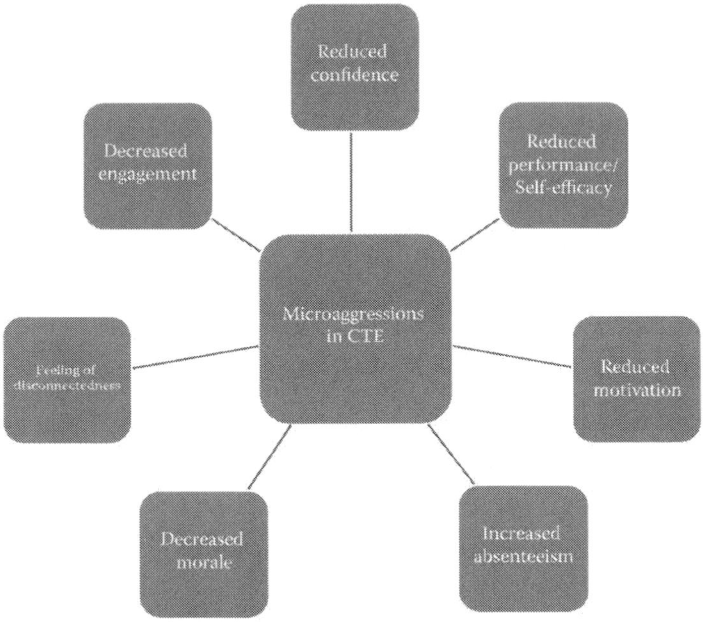

Teachers and school administrators should set the tone for positive academic communication. The way they communicate with and around students is enormously important. They should model the "what to" and "how to" of positive interactions. Unfortunately, it is not uncommon to see teachers employ microaggressive tactics in their academic interactions with students. This deviancy only reinforces microaggressions among students. In fact, teachers' actions, behaviors, demeanors, and temperaments play a significant role in determining how students behave in the classroom. Bailie (2015) argued that communication, engagement, presence, timeliness, responsiveness, and modeling positively affect online student satisfaction. These practices also apply to onsite student satisfaction. The content and form of teachers' communication have direct and indirect effects on students.

It is worth noting that students value being respected, trusted, accepted, listened to, and educationally empowered. Thus, teachers should tap into socio-affective factors that contribute to students' positive affect, such as joy, excitement, enjoyment, interest, and enthusiasm. Ultimately, praise, sense of humor, correction without rejection, encouragement, relationships, and social presence provide stimuli that can scaffold student engagement, creativity, resiliency, critical thinking skills, group harmony, instructional responsiveness, performance, resourcefulness, and CTE literacy. The essence of CTE teaching lies in this accomplishment. To be able to cope with microaggressions, student empowerment through education and dialogue is vital. Conversely, discourtesy, threats, overcorrection, harassment, sarcasm, and condescension can only lead to adversity and hostility.

Chapter 3

Empowerment Framework

Axial coding produced three critical success congruences in CTE environments: (a) psychological safety and student engagement congruence, (b) empowerment and microaggression deterrence congruence, and (c) equity and inclusion congruence. In other terms, a psychologically safe environment is positively associated with student engagement, higher efficiency, confidence building, and enhanced performance.

Microaggression deterrence through empowerment can lead to higher-quality CTE instruction. Finally, equity and inclusion can be intertwined to advance CTE learning. Figure 4 summarizes the relationships between the categories.

Figure 4. Conceptual Framework of CTE Instruction Success

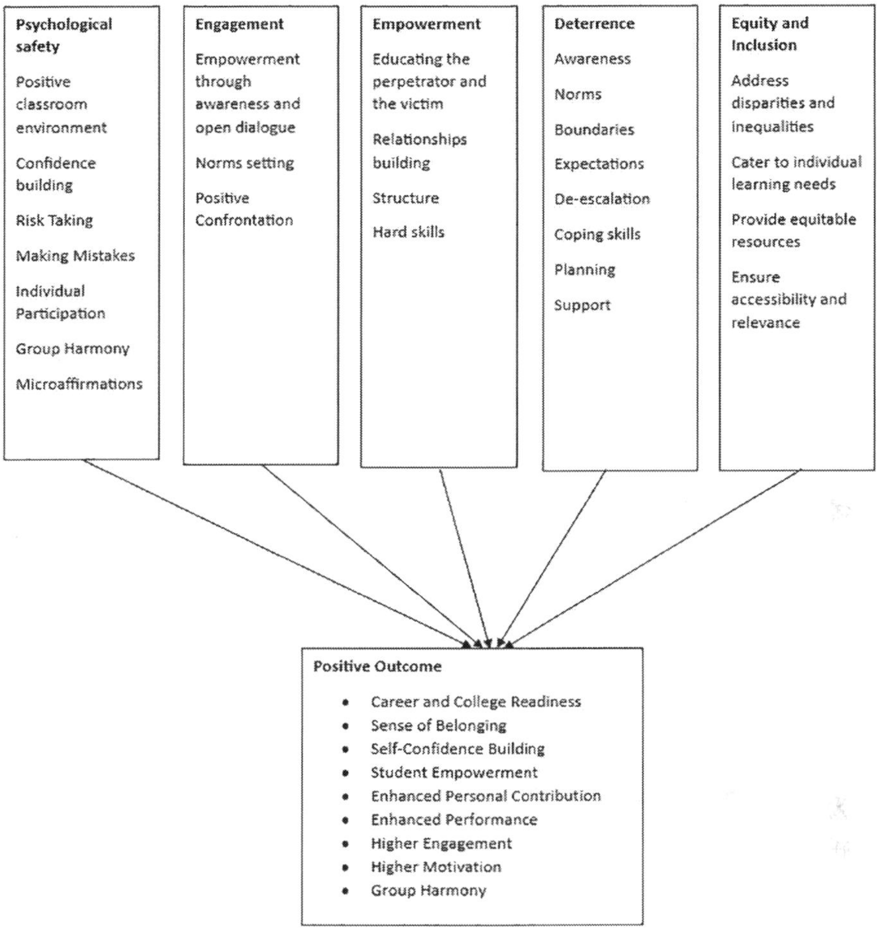

Psychological Safety and Engagement Congruence

It is widely recognized that disengagement is pervasive in schools (Corso et al., 2013). Psychological safety helps create conditions that positively affect student engagement and productivity. Desai et al. (2023) defined *psychological safety* as "a condition in which one feels safe to learn, contribute, and challenge the status quo without fear of being reprimanded, marginalized, or punished directly or indirectly" (p. 173). In essence, psychological safety enhances student engagement. Extant research lists motivation, relationships, structure, relevance of content, and teacher's expertise as contributing factors to student engagement and enhanced achievement in the classroom (Corso et al., 2013). Engagement can be achieved through setting clear norms and expectations, awareness and accountability, positive confrontation, microaffirmations, positive affect, and empowerment.

In short, psychological safety affects the quality of student engagement, learning outcomes, and teaching practices. This study establishes a congruence between psychological safety and student engagement. It establishes that a psychologically safe classroom environment helps students engage actively and holistically in learning endeavors and build confidence, as can be evidenced by these student quotes:

Sense of empowerment:

"Yes, I can accomplish anything when I feel trusted and respected" (Student 5).

"Yes, I would perform as best as I could; whether that is up to someone's standards is no concern of mine" (Student 15).

Responses to microaggressions differ. Not all students are impacted in the same manner. Responding to a question about how a microaggression incident affected students, some students indicated it never affected them, while others noted it affected them to some extent. One had mixed feelings:

Ambivalence regarding the impact of microaggressions:

"Yes and no. It made me believe that I did absolutely suck at that course. But also no, because I know I am bad at that course. So it did not really affect me much" (Student 7).

Accused of cheating on a CTE test by peers for being the first to finish, one student claimed the accusation did not affect him. Here is his response to whether the accusation affected his confidence:

Impact on self-confidence:

"Yes. A few days ago, we had a test in a CTE class. I was the first to finish and almost everyone thought I cheated. No, not really, because I knew that I didn't cheat" (Student 8).

While some thick-skinned students claimed to be unbothered by microaggressions, several argued that microaggressions impacted them negatively. In the following two examples, one thought she was not smart after experiencing a microinsult. Another noted that he stopped believing in himself.

Impact on self-confidence:

"It affected my confidence because I assumed that I was dumb for not meeting expectations" (Student 4)/

"It caused me to lack confidence in myself and I stopped believing in myself" (Student 11).

Conversely, some students are resilient and may not feel the immediate impact of microaggressions, as can be seen from the following statements:

Not impacted:

> "No, because I am not letting someone else ruin my confidence" (Student 54).
>
> "It didn't affect my confidence because I know I am capable of completing anything assigned to me, if explained well" (Student 52).

Ironically, not many students indicated that microaggressions affected them adversely. The following quotes illustrate that microaggressions can serve as confidence boosters for some students. These students felt rather incentivized by microaggression incidents.

Confidence boosting:

> "It honestly didn't affect my confidence since I've learned to ignore those types of people. In fact, it increased my confidence in showing off my work" (Student 51).
>
> "Yes, it made me more confident" (Student 55).

Student engagement is a powerful driver of student success (Bovill, 2020). Student engagement means CTE students are on task, engaged with instructional materials and activities focused on standards-based, integrated academics along with career-readiness skills (Castellano et al., 2014). Engaging learning is relevant, participatory, collaborative, and challenging. Students should be active participants in the learning process, interacting with the teacher, other students, and the content. Engaged CTE students should be actively involved in cooperative learning, problem-solving, creation and co-creation, design and decomposition, processing and meaning-making, investigating and creating, replicating and modifying, engineering and reverse engineering, designing and testing, analyzing and synthesizing, discussing and evaluating, interacting and hypothesizing, and sharing and reflecting. All these activities should require attention to detail, risk-taking, active listening, confidence building, mistake-making, meaningful social interaction, affective investment, critical learning skills, peer support, positive affect, microaffirmations, and tactful pedagogical facilitation. A psychologically safe environment is best suited for such endeavors. It is associated with student engagement, higher efficiency, and enhanced performance. It allows students to perform optimally.

Yet, empirical and anecdotal evidence reveals that one of the reasons students are not always fully engaged is ineffective instruction, leading to disturbances (Scott et al., 2014). It can be inferred that students' academic achievement, as well as teachers' performance, may suffer in an educational environment where adversity, hostility, toxicity, animosity, and mistrust are perpetually ubiquitous. The subsequent toxic climate may ultimately lead to conflict, verbal and physical confrontation, and inefficient learning outcomes. In CTE environments, a negative climate can amplify and exacerbate the effects of technostress, digital divide, inequity disparities, achievement gaps, and learning disabilities. Realistically, a classroom environment with microaggressions is not an ideal setting for active CTE learning or effective CTE teaching.

Without a classroom climate, optimal student engagement cannot be expected. It has emerged from data that a microaggressive environment can erode self-confidence; sow self-doubt; and negatively impact the ability of a student to participate in learning activities, volunteer to ask questions, take risks, make mistakes, speak up, propose new ideas, and share opinions without any fear of ridicule. Similarly, microaggressions can undercut a teacher's performance, mood, attitude, sense of self-worth, and self-efficiency. In other words, microaggressions can engender an environment that is not conducive to effective learning.

Student Empowerment and Microaggression Deterrence Congruence

Implicit bias develops at an early age, and microaggressions are the products of implicit bias, which may be hard to undo. The role of the teacher is crucial to help students unlearn microaggressive behaviors. As diverse groups of students come together, physically or virtually, they must learn to accept each other and treat each other with utmost respect. Hope and Timmel (1984) posited, "Unless there is this spirit of respect and acceptance, people will not be free to learn, to rethink their old opinions, to change and grow, or to share fully their thoughts and feelings" (p. 6). The feeling among students that their needs are recognized may be an important step toward activating a sense of ownership of the learning process. Because schools are quintessentially a microcosm of the real world, this sense of respect for self and others will carry over in every aspect of their lives beyond the classroom.

To minimize the occurrences of microaggressions and counter their negative effects, it is important to have preventive and responsive mechanisms in place through student empowerment. Student empowerment can be an effective means of equipping students with the appropriate skill set to become cocreators of learning and teaching. As partners of learning and teaching (Dunne, 2016; Mercer-Mapstone et al., 2017), students take greater initiative in the co-creation of a learning culture that fosters active participation, equity-mindedness, student engagement, shared decision-making, and personal responsibility. This implies meaningful collaboration between students and teachers (Bovill et al., 2016). As learning shifts from teacher-centered models to student-centered models, students should be empowered to take personal responsibility for the success of their own learning.

The skills required to deal with microaggressions are teachable and learnable (Dodge, 2019). Student empowerment entails adherence to a social contract outlining behavioral expectations in the classroom, as suggested by the Capturing Kids' Hearts program. It also entails students acquiring effective learning skills, which include academic skills, personal skills, and group interaction skills. Adapted from Howard High School of Technology's Quest for Quality Student Performance Guide (Bottoms & Sharpe, 1996), Table 4 summarizes these skills. Some skills have been modified, and new skills have been added. These skills help promote student engagement and a positive learning environment.

Table 4. Quest for Quality Student Performance Guide

Learning Skills for CTE Students		
Academic Skills	**Personal Skills**	**Group Skills**
Reading with understanding	Note-taking	Participating actively in groups
Understanding mathematics	Demonstrating self-control	Being sensitive to group members
Analyzing data	Demonstrating self-care	Compromising to reach goals
Problem-solving	Attending to details	Knowing group norms and standards
Self-expression	Following instructions	Listening to/observing group members
Addressing societal impacts of technology	Attending classes regularly	Knowing group members' names
Using, managing, and evaluating technology	Managing projects effectively	Expressing ideas to group members
Using research and library skills	Knowing personal strengths and weaknesses	Disagreeing without being disagreeable
Writing effectively	Uncovering one's biases and microaggressions	Working in changing environments

Learning Skills for CTE Students		
Academic Skills	**Personal Skills**	**Group Skills**
Speaking effectively	Responding to microaggressions with poise	Working with different demographics
Thinking creatively and critically	Verbalizing thoughts	Respecting others' ideas
Investigating and analyzing	Working independently	Leading or following to reach a goal
Drawing connections	Confronting a microaggression perpetrator	Collaborating with peers
Planning and designing	Demonstrating integrity, honesty, and respect	Providing feedback
Replicating, modifying, and creating	Developing career plans	Involving disinterested students
Using tools and equipment	Learning new skills	Assigning team roles
Providing feedback	Displaying creativity and imagination	Responding to questions
Deconstructing an object	Displaying loyalty	Time management
Encoding an object	Giving attention to quality	Accurately expressing one's ideas
Communicating/ presenting persuasively	Meeting school and work deadlines	Understanding an audience
Listening actively	Being properly groomed	Taking turns
Developing digital literacy	Dealing effectively with peers and microaggression perpetrators	Conflict management
Demonstrating leadership	Using judgment	Conflict resolution
Using resources productively	Goal setting	Effective negotiation
Innovating thinking	Demonstrating adaptability and flexibility	Solution-based strategic thinking

Learning Skills for CTE Students		
Academic Skills	**Personal Skills**	**Group Skills**
Technical writing	Demonstrating emotional intelligence	Building rapport and sharing
Programming	Receiving feedback	Decision making
Code review	Being detail-oriented	Accountability
Synthesizing and reflecting	Prioritizing tasks	Participating in group discussions

Dodge (2019) suggested a framework for handling difficult and uncomfortable conversations without being disagreeable. Students must be taught the virtues of positive confrontation, conflict resolution, social interaction, personal initiative, respect for self and others, active listening, and socialization. These traditional values contribute to making students effective communicators and sociable human beings, which affects the way they are perceived in society. If students learn to debate and convince persuasively with words, they are likely to engage in difficult conversations without being disagreeable, resolve conflict, and function appropriately in an academic setting. Hence, the primary goal is to create a learning environment that allows students to develop social interaction skills, intrapersonal skills, and interpersonal skills to solve authentic problems.

Positive Confrontation and Educational Empowerment

Open dialogue is vital to empower students to develop awareness of the context, content, and consequences of microaggressions. By allowing students to address instances of microaggressions through positive confrontation, teachers resolve to educationally empower students. Conversation is the cornerstone of a positive confrontation. A positive confrontation begins with an open, straightforward dialogue between a perpetrator who violates classroom norms and a victim who is subjected to microaggressions. The two parties should agree to discuss their genuine feelings and intentions in a respectful manner. They should agree to disagree and respect each other's point of view. They should not avoid talking about their biases and prejudices. However, they should focus on the positive aspects of the confrontation, which are mutual understanding, active listening, and compromise. They should agree on the purpose of the conversation: what to discuss, how to discuss, why to discuss, where to discuss, and who to involve. As Du Bois and Hutson (1997) observed, "Dialogue as an act of co-creation, therefore, is a matter of serious talk" (p. 43). Neither party should talk over the other, and both should decide if mediation is necessary. Once a resolution has been implemented, it should be evaluated and reevaluated to assess its effectiveness. Boundaries, norms, and expectations must be clearly defined. Any violation must be addressed.

If students run away from slights or microaggressions or passively confront them with silence or inaction, they are predisposing themselves to social dysfunction or inefficacy. Soft skills such as problem-solving, positive attitude, cross-cultural communication, active listening, goal-centric thinking, critical thinking, and compromising contribute to making students effective communicators, which can affect the way they are treated and perceived in society. Students must learn to verbalize specific thoughts or feelings, debate different viewpoints, articulate opinions, express frustrations, de-escalate conflict situations, and persuade with words or arguments. These skills can serve students positively when confronting microaggressions or other life challenges without resorting to verbal or physical violence. They can allow students to acknowledge personal biases, accept responsibility, empathize with victims, admit wrongdoing, and make amends. Thus, schools must help students learn to verbalize their thoughts, communicate specific feelings, and resolve conflicts peacefully.

A positive confrontation implies active listening, communication dexterity, and knowledge of the context. It is important to identify the place and time of the incident, the nature of microaggression, the audience, and the sociocultural background of the aggressor and the victim. This knowledge can help prevent or predict future occurrences. It is important that the two interlocutors address some critical points: perception of the incident, motivation and intent, reactions and feelings, and resolutions for the future.

A positive confrontation contributes to open communication and peaceful resolution of a conflict. Sue, Capodilupo, Torino, Bucceri, et al. (2007) proposed a five-phase model for deconstructing the microaggression process: (a) experience the incident; (b) attribute the aggressor's intent; (c) provide immediate cognitive, behavioral, and emotive reaction to the incident; (d) interpret and process the incident and reaction; and (e) proffer consequences of and consideration in coping with the microaggression.

As Lewis et al. (2013) pointed out, students' coping strategies are contingent upon the situation and contextual factors. Thus, individual personalities, personal relationships with the offender, and personal insecurities or vulnerabilities also influence the nature of the response. Therefore, a five-step approach to cope with microaggressions is adopted here: (a) identify a microaggression, (b) verify readiness to discuss, (c) have a positive confrontation, (d) have a resolution, and (e) evaluate the resolution.

The key to changing mindsets is the ability to identify microaggression. By nature, microaggressions are multifaceted and hard to deconstruct. As indicated earlier, they initially applied to only one racial group (Pierce et al., 1977). Their field has expanded to include religion, gender, socioeconomic status, ethnicity, nationality, sexual identity, and cultural background. They characteristically stem from a host of internal and external factors, namely, internalized prejudices, implicit biases, social stratification, standards of living, differential treatment, and lifestyle. The identification process is not an easy undertaking. Different conversational styles and cultural differences may lead to miscommunication that can be misconstrued as microaggressions.

Therefore, training is fundamental to the identification of microaggressive language and behaviors. Students and faculty must be trained in the characterization of microaggressions. Salient characteristics of microaggressions include the invisibility of bias; (un)awareness of the insult; trivialization of others' feelings, views, and contributions; and the offensive nature of the language or behavior. Here are a few guiding questions: Did a microaggression happen? What type of microaggression was it? When did it happen? Where did it happen? Why did it happen? Who was involved? How did it happen?

Another way to identify microaggressions is to administer a scale constructed to uncover microaggressions. Some of the commonly used instruments are the Student Microaggression Inventory (Berk, 2017a), Racial Microaggressions Scale (Torres-Harding et al., 2012), Gendered Microaggression Inventory (Yang & Carroll, 2016), Implicit Association Test (Greenwald et al., 1998), Homonegative Microaggressions Scale (Wright & Wegner, 2012), and Multidimensional Scale of Perceived Discrimination (Molero et al., 2013). Students should learn to identify patterns of microaggression and the underlying implicit bias that triggers them. They should be encouraged to document and report salient cases of microaggressions to teachers, school counselors, and school leaders. Once an identification is determined, the next step is to decide how to respond to a microaggression.

Ultimately, a positive confrontation does not need to occur on the same day as the incident because it can require some mental preparation. Preparation is key to the success of a positive confrontation. The victim and the aggressor must be ready to discuss in a good frame of mind, as presented in Figure 5. Given the confrontational nature of the encounter, a positive confrontation must be well thought out and well planned because it can turn into a chaotic verbal or physical altercation if it is not handled appropriately. An aggressive attitude may escalate the situation. To approach a perpetrator, the victim must be thoughtful and open to the eventuality of an agreement or a disagreement. By agreeing to disagree, an escalation can be prevented. It is important to remember that reasonable people can have reasonable differences. A good dose of humor can help defuse or de-escalate the situation. It may turn out that the aggressor had no intent to offend the victim. To curtail misunderstandings or miscommunications, instances of microaggressions must be approached and confronted strategically, pedagogically, and equitably.

Figure 5. Model of Microaggression Resolution

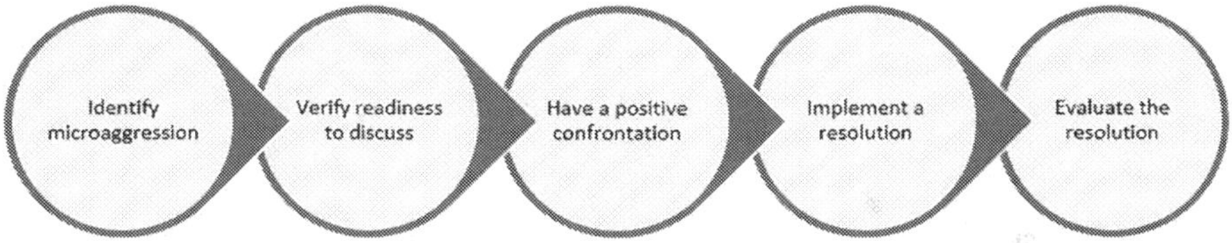

An effective resolution resulting from a positive confrontation is an agreement by both parties about the way forward. A resolution should begin with a review of the incident. The questions addressed earlier should be relevant here: What happened? Why did it happen? When did it happen? Where did it happen? Who was involved? What lessons can be learned from the incident? The offender must take the victim's feelings into account and make a commitment not to re-offend. This requires an introspective self-examination—looking deep into one's mind. Both parties, the aggressor and victim, must reexamine and challenge their implicit biases and their internalized prejudices. While it is practically impossible to be completely bias-depleted or prejudice-depleted, we can unlearn some of our biases and prejudices through self-knowledge.

Positive confrontation skills have known benefits that CTE classes need for operational effectiveness. They can help students and teachers restore relationships impacted by microaggressions. A few recommendations for restorative resources encompass Flippen's EXCEL Model from Capturing Kids' Hearts, Yale's RULER, and Restorative Practices (Costello et al., 2010, 2019; C. G. Vincent et al., 2016). The strength of positive confrontation rests on the following skills: assertiveness, attentive listening, persuasive speaking, spontaneity, receptiveness, and conflict resolution. These soft skills can increase self-confidence and decrease uncertainty, insecurity, and stress levels. Stevick (1990) postulated that humanistic education conditions can effectively amplify learning and provide an environment that facilitates the achievement of the full potential of the student. It is important that students, faculty, and school administrators frequently assess and reassess the way they communicate with peers and students.

Education as Deterrence Tactic

By default, conflict is embedded in the fabric of a diverse educational environment. The potential for conflict looms even larger in a classroom where microaggressions are prevalent. It is critically important that schools have management strategies in place to cope with microaggressions effectively. Failure to address microaggressions appropriately can adversely affect the psychological safety of all involved in the teaching and learning processes.

Deterrence alone is not enough. Having a coping mechanism to respond to microaggression occurrences through education and open dialogue empowers students and strengthens class cohesion, equity, inclusion, and student engagement. An educational component should be the centerpiece of any strategy to equip students with the appropriate skill set to respond to microaggressions calmly and assertively. Student empowerment has the potential to improve the classroom atmosphere and the learning culture. Students must also learn to be cognizant of their own biases and address them effectively. Dodge (2019) argued that eliminating microaggressions is a daunting challenge. However, students can use occurrences as opportunities for learning and change. Educating the offender, the victim, and the audience is a positive step toward student empowerment and toward deterrence. When students are equipped with soft skills to cope with microaggressions, they become more prepared and grow from the experience. All high-performing CTE classes have a certain level of conflict. What matters is knowing that students and teachers treat one another with respect, with dignity, with empathy, with fairness, and with honesty. They should be open-minded enough to acknowledge each other's feelings. The ultimate goal of a positive confrontation should be mutual understanding.

Knowing how to address microaggression incidents is important. Students respond to microaggressions in a variety of ways. Emotional responses may encompass nervousness, self-doubt, anxiety, stress, and tension. Some responses have been silence, inaction, violence (verbal or physical), confrontation, and compromise. When anxiety sets in, motivation sets out. Students must be taught how to regulate and manage emotions under certain stressful situations. Humor is a good coping strategy (Berk, 2015). Furthermore, silence, inaction, and passivity are ineffective responses to microaggressions. Sue (2015) contended, "The most ineffective strategies are [a] do nothing, [b] allow the discussion to be deflected away from the issue at hand, [c] shut down the discussion, and [d] exhibit defensive behaviors" (p. 231). These responses sow confusion and may promote biased behaviors and legitimize microaggressions

(Berk, 2017a; Sue et al., 2011). Ignoring a blatant instance of microaggression in the classroom to avoid a confrontation, exhibiting defensiveness, and changing the subject are not healthy strategies. A microaggression-permissive environment gives rise to several challenges, indicated earlier and as illustrated in Figure 6.

Figure 6. Model of Microaggression in a Permissive Classroom Environment

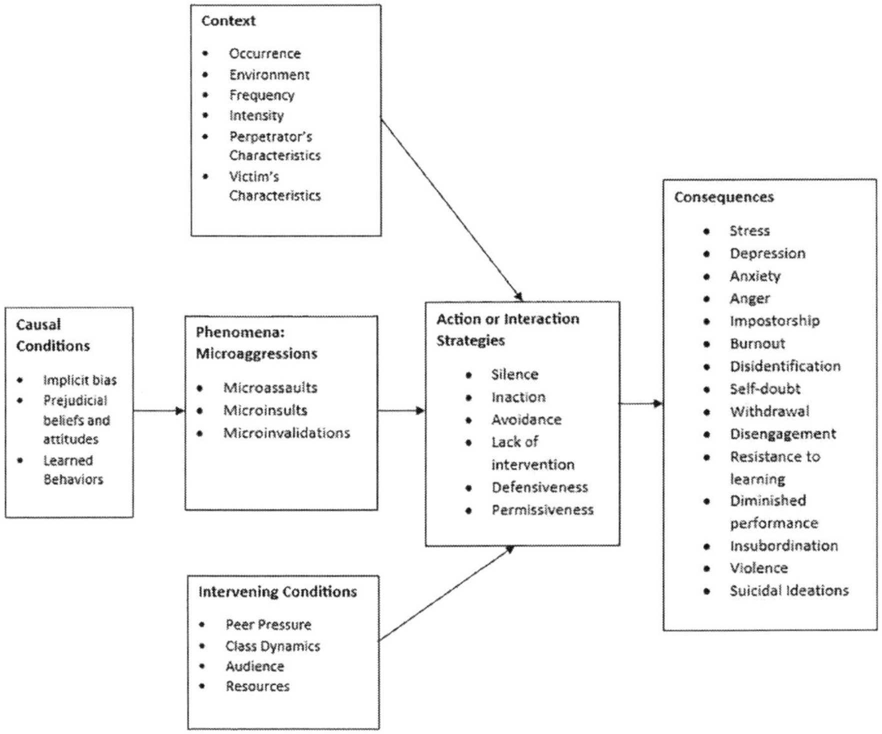

As noted earlier, students with social anxiety, stress, and low self-esteem may endure learning challenges because of microaggressive interactions. Some students may retaliate verbally or physically. A few may remain unaffected or may avoid confrontation by ignoring the incident or by changing the topic. Nathanson's (1992,

1997) Compass of Shame highlights four responses to inappropriate behavior: withdrawal, attack self, avoidance, or attack other. *Withdrawal* means isolating oneself and running and hiding. *Attack self* means self put-down and masochism. *Avoidance* includes denial, abusing drugs and alcohol, and distraction through thrill-seeking. *Attack other* involves turning the table, blaming the victim, and lashing out verbally or physically. Hynes (2008) indicated that individuals could resort to five possible conflict management strategies: avoiding, accommodating, compromising, problem-solving, and forcing. While students are encouraged to report incidents of microaggressions, it is important that they learn to manage them, to resolve them, and to confront them. Sue et al. (2019) suggested a micro-intervention framework for disarming microaggressions that comprises four strategic goals: (a) make the invisible visible, (b) educate the perpetrator, (c) disarm the microaggression, and (d) seek outside support and help.

Education, not sanctions, should be considered as a deterrent. It can be inferred that deterrence tactics minimize or counter the interference of microaggressions in CTE classrooms, thereby improving the quality of instruction and learning experiences. Therefore, a strategic plan to deter microaggressions preemptively must encompass an education component, an awareness protocol, a boundaries delineation protocol, a conflict management and resolution protocol, a de-escalation protocol, and coping mechanisms. A permissive environment is fertile ground for the adverse effects addressed earlier. Table 5 presents a theorized model of the harmful impact of microaggressions on students in a permissive classroom environment.

Responding to a microaggression with a microaggression is not a healthy option. It can turn into a ping-pong game with students throwing microaggressions at one another. Here are two illustrations:

Example 1:

A perfect example of a microaggression response to a microaggression occurred on *The O'Reilly Factor* on Fox News in 2010. Discussing President Obama's plan to reinforce the Mexican border, host Bill O'Reilly asked a question to Dr. Marc Lamont Hill, then-professor at Columbia University and political analyst, with a terrible microaggression: "Say you're a cocaine dealer. And you kind of look like one, a little bit."

The microaggression in the question seemed to startle some viewers. Dr. Hill responded with his own microaggression: "As do you! You look like a cocaine user." Luckily, this uncanny exchange on live television did not degenerate into a cacophonous argument or worse.

Example 2:

I personally faced a barrage of microaggressions from a young, white police officer in Nashville, Tennessee on March 14, 2014. I drove to that beautiful city for the first time to attend my doctoral commencement ceremony which was scheduled for March 15, 2014 at 10:00 in the morning. Upon my arrival, I checked in to a hotel around 3:30 in the afternoon. Roughly half an hour later, I left the hotel for the Music City Center, which was the commencement ceremony venue, to register for the event. I exited the highway several minutes later to purchase some snacks. Soon after I got off the highway, an unmarked police vehicle abruptly made a left turn with its siren on. I pulled over and made a blunder of getting out of my then six-month old vehicle. This led the young, tattooed police officer to sternly order me to get back in my vehicle. This was my first police stop in the United States.

"What seems to be the problem, officer?" I politely queried when he came by my car door after patiently checking my vehicle license plate. "You are driving fast in a school zone," he replied, adding: "You are going 30 miles per hour in a 15-mile school zone! Don't you have schools where you are coming from?" The officer assumed that I had no idea what a school zone looked like. Little did he know that I was a veteran, master teacher with over a decade of teaching experience in the United States and another decade overseas. There were no school traffic signs in the vicinity and no flashing lights urging drivers to limit speed to 15 miles per hour. Moreover, there were no students around and the time was between 4:00 and 4:30 in the afternoon. The police officer took my driver's license to his vehicle and returned a few minutes later. I showed him my graduation documents which justified my visit to the city. He reluctantly allowed me to leave after scolding me for driving at the same speed as other drivers behind and in front of me.

Several months later, I called his precinct to inquire about the unusual traffic stop. I found out that the facts of the case were misrepresented. "The stop occurred at 51st Avenue N and Indiana Avenue at 0042 hours on 3/15/14," the report stated. As a matter of fact, the stop occurred on March 14, 2014 between 4:00 pm and 4:30 pm. His supervisor stated that there was a school about four blocks away. I asked the name of the school and was told to "Google it." Google it, I did. I did not find it.

Responding to the officer with poise spared me of unwanted drama and allowed me to leave without an incident. I complied with his request to show my driver's license. I also did not question his motive for stopping me. Yet, I knew, deep down, that it was unfounded. However, I did dispute the incident report and was told that it would be difficult to come to any resolution regarding what had occurred since there had been such a delay in reporting the incident.

Example 3:

A half-Hispanic, half-Arab student told a joke that left his classmates confused. “You know what happened yesterday?” he began.

“What happened?” another student asked.

“Two slave ships crashed and caused an oil spill.” He continued jokingly, laughing out loud, “So the Red Sea became the Black Sea!”

Some students laughed. Others were left perplexed. An African-American student interjected disapprovingly, “How long have you been a racist?”

The young man replied, “Someone taught me that joke in middle school.” He went on to say, “I am not a racist. I only do it to be funny. If I was a racist, do you think I would attend this school? I only say these things for laughs. They help me test your level of tolerance.”

The class had Asian students, Hispanic students, White students, and African-American students. As a response to this horrendous joke, a Hispanic student asked him, “Is your father, Osama bin Laden? Are you a terrorist?” The class laughed. The young man who started the joke did not.

In many cases, students think they are only joking and their jokes are harmless. However, their words and behaviors may have serious consequences. Teachers deal with similar situations on a regular basis. Here is an example of a student-to-teacher microaggression:

Example 4:

A Hispanic student was teasing his African teacher, asking him if he used to walk around naked when he was growing up in Africa, like some tribes he watched in a documentary about Africa. He asked jokingly, "Do you have schools in Africa? I heard you did not wear clothes when you were in Africa!"

The teacher tried to use the opportunity as a teaching moment. However, the student was not in the mood for a lecture. After a constant barrage of unpleasant jokes about Africa, the teacher asked the student if he knew anything about the underexplored tribes of the Amazon because the student reminded the teacher of a video he had watched about those beautiful tribes. The student's laughter quickly turned into fury, with the class now laughing at him. The situation almost got out of control. The teacher explained to the students why it was important to listen and not to degrade a category of people. The student remained quiet and was visibly upset.

Example 5:

A terrible joke went wrong. A female student asked for permission to go to the restroom. She did not lock her computer. While she was away, an African American boy, who suspected the young lady of being a lesbian, replaced her screensaver with a large photograph of two ladies having sexual intercourse. He knew how to circumvent school restrictions about suggestive materials. The entire class saw the screensaver. Most of the students laughed profusely. When the young lady returned, the class was still laughing. She saw the screensaver and was very upset. Full of rage, she asked, "Who did this?" She was ready for a fight. Unfortunately, nobody told her who the culprit was. The substitute teacher called a security associate to handle the chaos that ensued.

Teachers must be brave enough to firmly tackle these incidents. They must possess the right set of skills and techniques because microaggressions can have short-term, mid-term, and long-term effects on students' productivity and morale. Similarly, students must be equipped with skills and knowledge to diffuse potential microaggressive conflicts. They are expected to have uncomfortable conversations with their peers. Therefore, they must understand the virtues and benefits of positive confrontation.

Overcoming Mental Barriers

A major barrier to the learning process is a learner's mental disposition, which can suppress or negatively impact the drive, motivation, competence, and ability to learn. *Mental barriers,* as they are known, are psychological, perceptual, emotional, intellectual, environmental, instructional, and sociocultural in nature. It is quite commonplace to hear students express defeatist attitudes toward their cognitive capabilities regarding certain courses that they deem to be too complex or too hard. They erect mental blocks that may become obstacles in the long run for achieving academic success, leading to depression and anxiety. These mental barriers can impede student academic achievement (Panayiota, 2022). Hence, students need to be equipped with skills to deal with these mental obstacles that can impact their academic performance in addition to the academic skills, personal skills, and collaboration skills highlighted earlier. Students should be active participants who can identify and overcome any systemic mental barriers that impede their learning.

Several students shared disparaging statements about their own cognitive abilities to learn. It is assumed that the statements are expressions of attitudes rather than actual aptitudes. Table 5 summarizes statements made by CTE students that include negative self-image, aversive phobia, fear and defensiveness, false inference, underestimation of personal abilities, and perceptions and viewpoints. These feelings can be serious obstacles to active learning. They shape mindsets and attitudes in the classroom.

Table 5. Summary of Mental Barriers

Theme	Quote
Negative self-image	• "I give up. I don't have patience for this stuff." • "This is not my thing." • "I already know that I am going to fail. I don't know this stuff." • "This is too hard." • "I am dumb." • "I am stupid." • "I know I will fail this class."
Aversion	• "I used to be good in math, but I lost interest because I don't like my math teacher." • "This is not a math class. Why are we doing math in this class? I suck at math." • "I skip that class because I don't like the teacher." • "Let's all fail so that the teacher can be fired! You know teachers can be fired if their students don't do well!"
False inference	• "I am not going to do well in this class because I am not good with computers, and I don't like computers." • "I am not good with computers. I don't like computer classes."
Fear and defensiveness	• "I did not sign up for this class." • "I am never going to use this, anyway." • "I don't need this class to graduate." • "You expect too much of us." • "I don't care about this class; I am not going to college, anyway."

Theme	Quote
Underestimation of one's personal abilities	• "I am not creative." • "I will never be anything in life." • "I am not artistic." • "Math is not my thing." • "I can't draw." • "Don't expect me to have a good grade; I don't do well on tests. I am not a good test taker."
Perceptions and viewpoints	• "All I need is a C to pass this class. I am not going to college. You don't need to go to college to be successful. Bill Gates dropped out of college. *Mark Zuckerberg dropped out! Steve Jobs dropped out, too! You are not going to convince me to change my mind. College is not for me!*" • "I never study before an exam; I am not Asian." • "You know I am from the ghetto. This is how we talk."
Self-exclusion	• "I am not going to join a team; I am not a team player. I work by myself."

If anything, these statements invoke a psychological hurdle that can be attributable to an array of factors such as self-doubt, uncertainty, fixed mindset, indecision, disinterest, fear of the unknown, lack of focus, lack of persistence or resilience, teacher-phobia, and learning disability. These mental blocks can indeed inhibit a learner's cognitive capacity or academic performance. Bandura and Locke (2003) observed that such negative emotions and attitudes can rob students of their abilities to learn new things. While positive beliefs play a motivational role in boosting student motivation and performance, negative beliefs are incapacitating, negatively interfering with the process of learning. Early life experiences, past educational experiences, peer pressure, and family influences often affect how students react in the face of educational challenges. Research consistently shows that students with a positive growth mindset often outperform students with a negative, fixed mindset.

Efficacy beliefs are significantly correlated with the level of motivation and performance (Bandura & Locke, 2003).

Positive experiences can be motivating. When I was a child, my father envisioned that I would be a medical doctor. He believed that I had what it would take to become a physician, so much so that he used to call me "doctor." He passed away when I started elementary school. Some of my siblings continued to call me "doctor." Unfortunately, I was not lucky enough to be admitted to a medical school even though I tried hard (my concentration in high school was biochemistry). More importantly, I was so motivated to earn a doctoral degree in any field to honor my father's wish. And I did. While intrinsic motivation was a key factor, extrinsic motivation also played a significant part. Thus, encouragement from teachers, peers, parents, and the community at large contributes to student performance enhancement.

Mental blocks may also be by-products of personal experiences. It is important to praise students for their abilities rather than scold them for their inabilities or deficiencies. A student once reported, "My third-grade teacher told me that I could only spell 10 words! That bothered me for a long time." Such words as "dumb," "stupid," "big baby," "nigger," "knucklehead," "imbecile," "wet bag," and "butthead" that students reported hearing from peers, teachers, or parents may have a profound psychological impact. A teacher confided that one of her first-grade students was surprised that she called him by his last name because his mother called him the N-word so often that he came to believe it was his name. Parents and teachers who denigrate youngsters may never realize how cognitively debilitating their denigrations can be. They should refrain from insulting and devaluing children's intelligence. In CTE environments, name-calling should have no place. Many students have had negative learning experiences that have shaped their beliefs about learning. They believe their abilities to learn a subject have stagnated or dissipated. This belief is erroneous. Educators must challenge students to take risks and to reexamine their limits. This may not be an easy process because it means that educators must believe in their students and provide the support they need.

How to end mental blocks is an open question. Several scholars have offered insights on this topic. First and foremost, it is important to identify the mental block. Once identified, it should be handled efficiently and effectively. Mueller (2019) suggested four strategies: uncover the causes, remove the blocks, reduce their power, and transform the blocks. Essentially, uncovering the causes of mental blocks involves the following steps: knowing your values, asking why, finding examples, and looking for conflicts. Removing the blocks involves a systematic three-step process: recording the monologues, tracing the source, and requiring evidence. If followed, these steps can result in the elimination or reduction of mental blocks that slow down students. To reduce the power of mental blocks, it is critical to talk about them and take action. Given the fact that any teaching is judged in terms of the learning that results from it, it is vital that teachers explore various tools at their disposal to help students overcome their mental blocks. The fewer, the merrier.

Gradually changing students' perceived weaknesses to actual strengths can help refocus attention on what can be accomplished rather than on what cannot be accomplished. A can-do mindset is a significant asset. The reexamination of strengths and weaknesses should foster a rekindling of the learning commitment. With a change of heart and attitude, students may undertake an appropriate course of action that can lead to positive results. Actions can encompass revisiting learning strategies, acquiring new study skills, recommitting time and effort, prioritizing learning activities versus entertainment, exploring other forms of intelligence, and approaching learning tasks differently. The focus should be on what is positive rather than what is negative, on what is possible rather than what is impossible, and on what is attainable rather than what is unattainable.

Teacher Role in Unblocking Mental Barriers

It is the teacher's professional duty to lead students to reexamine and challenge their attitudes, their thoughts, and their limits—perceived or real. A perceived weakness may not be a weakness at all. It may be caused by a fixed mindset. Sometimes a change in attitude, in teaching style, or in learning approach may rekindle a learner's interest in a subject or a desire to approach a learning activity differently. Students need a growth mindset, a can-do mindset about their learning capabilities. To instill a growth mindset, educators need to shift their discourse from inability to ability. Students will develop a positive attitude if educators emphasize what students can do rather than what they cannot do. Students need to hear the following statements from their teachers:

> "You can do it. Math is easy."
>
> "Programming is fun and useful."
>
> "This course is not hard."
>
> "It does not matter whether you are right or wrong, just do it."
>
> "You are one of the smartest students I know. You can do this."
>
> "You probably do not realize how creative you are!"
>
> "I know you are going to pass the test."
>
> "Coding is not always easy. It requires hard work. You may fail if you do not do the work that is needed! But with the right mindset, you will do well."
>
> "Don't underestimate yourself. You are capable of completing this task!"

A positive relationship between an educator and a student can serve as a catalyst for the process. It can produce many positive opportunities for lifelong learning. Educators need to know their students and build positive relationships with them. Getting to know students implies reviewing student records through student information systems, talking to parents and school counselors, and conducting needs assessments.

Here is an example of a teacher who led a student to change her mind about test taking. The female African-American student was unwilling to take a mock exam or retake it because she already knew she would fail. She claimed that she hated the class. She said, "I don't do well on tests. You don't understand. I can retake this test and still fail." The student's grade for her first attempt was 76%. She refused to retake the test. After the teacher failed to convince her to retake the test, he threatened to call the student's father and tell him that his daughter said she was okay with a C. Fearing her father's reaction, the student finally agreed to retake the test after reviewing her notes. In other words, she approached the test differently. Her second attempt grade was 86%. "Who said you could not do well?" the teacher asked. The student simply smiled and said, "I did not know I could do that well. I think I can even do better than this if I take it again. Can you reset the test for me, please?" The teacher let her take it again and this time she scored 96%.

In another example: A parent of a CTE student called a teacher around 9:00 in the evening. He introduced himself and asked if his daughter could retake a test for Scientific and Technical Visualization I. The teacher was surprised because the student's first score was 92%, but he agreed. The student scored 100% on her second attempt. How many parents act like this? Some students were asked what their parents would have done. There were mixed responses: "92% is an A; why retake?" "My father would have never called you about that!" "That man must be crazy!" "He must be Asian!" In fact, the father was from India.

With literacy development as the primary goal, students should be taught to read, write, listen, and speak. Hartley and Viney (1982) explained that students learn by doing: "People learn to listen by listening. People learn to speak by speaking. People learn to read by reading. People learn to write by writing" (p. 7). Thus, it is important that teachers teach some common learning strategies and skills, including (but not limited to):

1. note taking,
2. active listening,
3. oral presentation,
4. decision making,
5. formalized routines,
6. organization and research,
7. inspectional or active reading (skimming, annotating, clustering, group reading),
8. making educated guesses,
9. role playing,
10. debating,
11. analyzing and synthesizing,
12. hypothesis making and testing,
13. concept mapping,
14. problem-solving,
15. brainstorming,
16. drawing conclusions,
17. summarizing,
18. probing,
19. questioning,
20. group collaboration,
21. teamwork,

22. being responsive,
23. written and verbal communication,
24. creative writing,
25. evaluating,
26. strategizing,
27. consensus seeking,
28. social interaction,
29. positive confrontation,
30. active participation,
31. punctuality,
32. anticipation,
33. open dialogue, and
34. time management.

Gamification can be used to incentivize students to learn some of these study skills. Ultimately, learning outcomes may be hard to measure because the impact of such an investment may not always be felt immediately. However, this investment should yield short-term, mid-term, and long-term results. Therefore, teachers should teach a broad range of study skills and learning strategies to guide the learning process. For example, if students are taught how to avoid academic procrastination, it is unlikely they will be procrastinators. Lack of proper study skills is one of the causal factors of student failure and unpreparedness for college course loads.

Thus, the centrality of education in student empowerment is undeniable. It has a deterrent effect on microaggression occurrences. The more educated students are about the harmful effects of microaggressions, the less likely they are to commit microaggressions. Student empowerment through education and dialogue can help students gain control of the classroom dynamics, resulting in enhanced learning experiences. Kirk et al. (2016) postulated that intrapersonal student empowerment is a predictor of positive outcomes in the classroom, namely, a sense of community, discipline, academic achievement, extracurricular activity involvement, and heightened educational aspirations. As Palloff and Pratt (2001) convincingly argued, "In order for a high degree of interactivity to occur in a course, faculty need to let go of the control of the course and empower students to take responsibility for the learning process" (p. 3). Taking ownership of the learning process helps students partake in the give-and-take interplay.

Leveraging students' intellectual capital, teachers should lead students to critically assess their own biases. It is critical for CTE teachers to raise their students' understanding of the causes, manifestations, and consequences of microaggressions that permeate their learning environments. Students should also learn to respond to microaggressions calmly and assertively. An asset-based approach, not a deficit-based approach, is critical for distributed leadership development, equitable teacher-learner relationships, and shared decision-making. P. Vincent and Grove (2013) offered a working formula for educational success: Relationships + Rules + Routines = Results. They postulated that relationships built between students and teachers through engagement can be efficient drivers of self-efficacy (P. Vincent & Grove, 2012, 2013). Given the clear advantages of student engagement and the high costs of student disengagement, teachers should take advantage of any strategy that can help generate enhanced engagement. Student engagement is said to be associated with heightened learning, while disengagement is known to lead to discipline problems.

Escalation/De-escalation

Teachers are trained to handle discipline problems in the classroom. However, there can never be enough reminders about de-escalation strategies. Teachers must be constantly reminded to de-escalate conflict situations. Several instances of teachers verbally reacting to students' threats with their own threats have been reported. They do not want to appear weak. They raise their voices, move toward students, and use emotionally charged words that may trigger an emotional or angry response. It is important to remember that violence breeds violence, anger breeds anger, and staying calm has a calming effect. Name-calling, sarcasm, insults, threats of violence, and physical contact may escalate a situation. Teachers should avoid using the following sentences:

"I do not want to hurt you."

"What are you going to do?"

"Go ahead, do what you want to do and you will find out."

"You are not going to do anything about it."

"Man, I swear to God."

"Boy, you are too small for me."

"Show me what you got."

"Do something!"

"I need your hands."

"I have fast hands."

"Do not let this suit fool you."

"Do you want to square up?"

"Do you want to scrap?"

"Do you want to fight?"

"Get out of my face."

"I am not going to warn you again."

"You are nothing but a baby."

"I will deal with you as if I own you."

"I am too quick for you."

These sentences may challenge students to react with their own threats or worse, with violence. Students do not like to appear weak in front of an audience of their peers. Moreover, teachers should avoid referring to students as "coward," "thug," "ghetto," "taco boy," "bastard," "nigger," "cracker," "whip," "loser," "dirty," "coon," "pound," "wet bag," and similar words. They may trigger an emotional response, enticing students to react aggressively.

Theoretical Elements in Student Empowerment

> Authentic education is not carried on by "A" for "B" or by "A" about "B," but rather by "A" with "B," mediated by the world—a world which impresses and challenges both parties, giving rise to views and opinions about it. These views, impregnated with anxieties, doubts, hopes, or hopelessness, imply significant themes or the basis on which the program content of education can be built. (Freire, 1968/1972, p. 82)

Several studies have highlighted theoretical frameworks that can influence student empowerment and affect dynamic interactions between teacher and learner in an educational environment. Social–emotional learning theory (Jones & Doolittle, 2017), social learning theory, social impact theory (Latané, 1981), and cognitive–affective–social theory of learning in digital environments (Schneider et al., 2022) are four relevant examples. Elements of each theory can illuminate the student educational empowerment process. Student empowerment is about capacity building. Student empowerment entails positive confrontation, soft skills, de-escalation, education, restorative practices, conflict resolution, and acknowledging feelings. In short, it means building relational capacity (releasing the "power within" and giving the "power to" and the "power with" students to self-manage).

Naturally, a student's educational empowerment is contingent upon the pedagogical and psychological actions of a variety of sources (or social actors). To optimize the effectiveness of the teaching process—and consequently improve the CTE quality of learning—and to exert an influence on the dyadic teacher–learner relationship, the impact should be subject to credibility, mutual trust, open-mindedness, receptiveness, and respect. On the one hand, a teacher's expertise, experience, pedagogical skills, instructional leadership, and responsiveness are deemed to be critical predictors of student success. On the other hand, a student's intrinsic motivation, goal setting, academic resilience, and discipline are important enablers of academic achievement. The combination of these factors is likely to result in a more efficient give-and-take interplay. In fact, it is not the number of people that students interact with at school that affects them the most, it is the quality of stakeholders: a caring school counselor, a charismatic school leader, an effective teacher, a supportive parent, and so forth.

Clearly, the power of the educator as an influencer or behavior modeler does not necessarily derive from their level of education attainment, age, race, or gender. However, demonstrated empathy, proven expertise, and experience may partially account for the influence teachers can exert on students. The immediacy of the source is the closeness in time and space between the influencer and the learner. This closeness can be physical, virtual, or psychological. An impactful teacher's influence does not end in the confines of the classroom's physical space. It goes beyond the bounds of the classroom walls and the school campus. A student may remember a teacher's motivational thought, a study skill learned in class, a joke, an expectation, a coping strategy, and so forth. The people (teacher, teacher assistant, academic facilitator, counselor, assistant principal, and principal) in the educational environment of the learner may account for the magnitude of the impact. The influencing source can affect the student's perception and reception of course content or target performance skills. Although the number of sources does not matter, it appears that the more sources of influence there are, the greater the chances of an impact. The more role models there are in the life of a learner, the more likely the impact will be positive. Students are often more receptive and open to knowledge shared by credible, trustworthy, and knowledgeable educators or school administrators. The process can result in strengthened and enhanced student performance. Therefore, a student's satisfaction with an educator has been linked to academic achievement.

However, student dissatisfaction is often linked to a stressful learning environment and experience. Research shows that underperforming students may regard a stressful educational setting and the learning process as a source of anxiety (Cipriano & Brackett, 2020), which can be conducive to decreased self-efficacy, engagement, motivation, and connectedness. Students' social-emotional health must be an integral part of CTE curricula. Disregarding this aspect can have adverse repercussions on students. Also, recruiting and retaining effective teachers must be a leadership goal.

Implications for Practice

The results of this investigation provide some insightful, introspective opportunities for teachers. First, it has been established that teachers can diminish or limit their own effectiveness by allowing microaggressions to interfere with their teaching. Teachers must be cognizant of the negative consequences of microaggressions on their own performance as well as on their students' cognitive, affective, emotional, and mental health. Results of inaction, avoidance, silence, inattention, and passivity on their part encompass, among other consequences, withdrawal, disengagement, instructional unresponsiveness, insubordination, phobia, self-doubt, verbal and physical confrontation, inefficient and ineffective performance, resistance to learning, tuning out, frustration, and anger. Subsequently, these effects can ultimately lead to public humiliation, lack of participation, sleep disorder, and suicidal ideations.

Second, teachers can undermine their own effectiveness by creating an unwelcoming learning environment in which microaggressions have free rein. The classroom atmosphere that results from confrontational social interactions can have profound negative consequences. Deborah Tannen (1998), a well-known sociolinguist who has published a great deal of research on cross-cultural communication, noted that the argument culture creates "an adversarial frame of mind" (p. 3) that rests on opposition. In an adversarial classroom environment, there is little or no trust between teachers and students. Thus, students will not fully bring themselves into a classroom where they can be ridiculed, demoralized, or dehumanized or where they are compelled to follow a teacher-prescribed agenda. Teacher performance will ultimately suffer in this context.

To unlock students' true academic potential, teachers must acknowledge their values, aspirations, needs, views, fears, dreams, doubts, preferences, experiences, memories, goals, hobbies, and personal and academic interests. They should avoid subjugating students into submission with condescending attitudes and negativity in their daily discourse and behaviors because coercive compliance can only lead to a microaggressive classroom environment. Such an environment plants seeds of a dysfunctional classroom. In other words, a teacher's sarcasm, moodiness, and microaggressions negatively affect the classroom atmosphere. Teachers must watch their body language, the tone of their voice, and the words they use. To check one's inner biases, a teacher must work on reducing and eliminating instances of microaggressions in their classroom. They should be encouraged to foster an active learning environment based on core educational values, namely, mutual respect, can-do mindset, communication, collaboration, risk-taking, and active participation. Such an environment values diversity, resiliency, and high performance. It is incumbent upon teachers to facilitate the learning process by creating conditions that nurture the emotional, mental, cognitive, and intellectual development of students.

Teachers' attitudes usually shape and influence the dynamic of classroom interactions. For students who have been historically exposed to various types of indignities due to their race or socioeconomic status, it is unwise to exacerbate their negative feelings in the classroom. Some students face a host of challenges, including homelessness, extreme poverty, absence of a parent or parents, residential mobility, or learning disabilities. It is the teacher's primary responsibility to create an instructionally supportive and safe environment for every student.

Additionally, the impact of classroom microaggressions on teacher performance can be significant. Microaggressive teachers may limit their own effectiveness. Their power to facilitate the learning process can be called into question, negated, rejected, or discredited. In fact, teachers' underperformance can be partly attributable to classroom climate, among other factors. To encourage students to become active learners and productive cocreators of knowledge, teachers must create an open, respectful atmosphere that is conducive to effective learning. Microaggressions from students, colleagues, and administrators can contribute to raising teachers' stress levels.

Job satisfaction is known to be a key pillar of teacher retention. The more satisfied teachers are, the more likely they are to remain in their jobs. Ambiguity, bureaucracy, and work overload can heighten teacher stress, leading some teachers to quit. Teachers reported that teacher pay, students' behaviors, job dissatisfaction, and lack of instructional support are the four main reasons why they needed another line of work.

Finally, the link between microaggressions and productivity suggests that microaggressions can create stress, anxiety, and pedagogical hypertension. In other words, microaggressions can engender an environment that is not conducive to effective and affective learning. By implementing microaggression management strategies, teachers can reduce conflicts, negative verbal altercations, and physical altercations.

Conclusion

Clearly, the pervasiveness of microaggressions in a CTE environment articulates a malaise. The resulting paralyzing dysfunction can significantly hamper student achievement and teacher effectiveness. As a facilitator of the learning process, the teacher's pedagogical responsibility is to create conditions that ultimately lead to active learning and not impede the learning process, by allowing a culture of microaggressions in the classroom. In effect, emphasis should be placed on an educated understanding of the benefits of inclusion, equity, surface-level or demographic diversity (age, race, ethnicity, religion, gender, socioeconomic status, sexual orientation, physical ability, and cultural background), and deep-level diversity (cultural values, communication styles, preferences, attitudes, and personalities) in a CTE environment. Diversity should be acknowledged, celebrated, and exploited strategically. Limited English proficiency, for example, should not be viewed as ignorance, nor should a student or teacher be judged based on skin color, zip code, state or country of origin, religion, or gender. Physical presence, personal qualities, class attendance, and CTE literacy must be valued and celebrated.

It is important that teachers and students develop informed awareness of appropriate management strategies to reduce or manage incidents of microaggressions in the classroom or on school grounds. It can be surmised from the study findings that consistently educating the perpetrator and the victim, setting boundaries, using humor, providing and encouraging students to seek support, using positive affect, having an array of microaggression management protocols in place, and engaging students in open dialogue are effective tactics that can have positive consequences. Those consequences include (but are not limited to) a positive classroom atmosphere, course participation, instructional responsiveness, compliance with rules, trust building, positive confrontation, effective performance, active learning, leadership emergence and consolidation, soft-skills empowerment, and hard-skills development and consolidation.

CTE teachers should ensure that students harness employability skills and college readiness skills and are prepared to face real-world, societal challenges. Student educational empowerment is paramount to student engagement. There should be open discussions about the need to reduce or eliminate instances of microaggressions. Biases of all kinds must be acknowledged, addressed, and handled accordingly. The failure to address the pervasiveness of microaggressions and their harmful impact on student achievement and teacher performance can only perpetuate a culture of prejudice. The ability of students, instructors, and school administrators to treat one another with respect increases the potential for educational success.

Microaggressions have traditionally been recognized as impediments to active learning. Several studies have highlighted their effects on teaching and learning processes. However, there is a dearth of comprehensive studies in the field of STEM, despite the increasing attention this topic has received. The current study aimed to critically examine the nature of microaggressions within the realm of CTE instruction to uncover their effects and to suggest a framework to minimize their interference in a CTE classroom with the ultimate goal of improving CTE instruction. The grounded theory study focused on two types of congruence that can enhance the quality of CTE instruction: (a) psychological safety and engagement congruence and (b) student empowerment and microaggression deterrence congruence. Based on the results of data analysis, it was surmised that a psychologically safe environment is positively associated with enhanced efficacy and student success. Deterrence through educational empowerment and positive confrontation aids in minimizing the interference of microaggressions in CTE classrooms. The suggested student empowerment framework calls for additional research for empirical validation. Further exploration of the framework with different methodological approaches and target populations can help confirm the study findings.

To conclude, this section explored the multifaceted nature of microaggressions in CTE classrooms from the points of view of teachers and students. It established that microaggressions create a hostile learning environment that can adversely affect the psychological safety of all involved in the teaching and learning processes. Such an environment can amplify and exacerbate the effects of technostress, academic underachievement, ineffective performance, digital divide, and inequity. Microaggressions should not be normalized because they constitute barriers to student learning, academic achievement, group harmony, equity, and inclusion. Eliminating microaggressions altogether is a nearly impossible task. However, minimizing their interference in classroom dynamics is possible. Empowerment through education and dialogue is key to curbing the frequency, intensity, and occurrence of microaggressions. Proper management tactics help reduce stress and anxiety. Fundamentally, it is crucial for schools to review and rethink some of their policies to ensure effective instruction and learning for all students.

SECTION 2

Fueling Organizational Performance and Instructional Effectiveness

Introduction

This section explores how a blended model of educational leadership in conjunction with heightened awareness of drivers and inhibitors of active learning and effective leadership can fuel organizational and instructional effectiveness. Taken together, the three chapters in this section employ a selective, macro-theoretical approach to leadership rather than a single model approach, drawing on elements of multiple leadership models and addressing a variety of topics to improve instructional efficacy.

Chapter 4, "A Blended Model of Educational Leadership," examines the content of effective leadership, factors affecting educational leadership (such as halo effect, Hawthorne effect, bias, and in-group and out-group), shared leadership, and strategic leadership. It highlights a multi-dimensional model based on theoretical elements of several leadership models. It begins with why effective educational leadership matters. Next, it discusses factors affecting effective leadership and transitions to shared leadership and strategic leadership. It ends with a conclusion.

Chapter 5, "Drawing from Other Models of Leadership," explores theoretical elements that can be drawn from other models of leadership, including transformational leadership, transactional leadership, leader-member exchange theory, and trait theories. It highlights some beneficial elements that can be drawn from each leadership model and warns against differential treatment of employees based on in-group and out-group establishment. It ends with a conclusion.

Chapter 6, "Improving Instruction Quality and Managing Diversity," discusses drivers and inhibitors of student learning, the importance of knowing students, strategies for overcoming mental obstacles, the link between teacher talk and student language fossilization, and the intricacies of teaching in the United States as an immigrant. It also advocates for small-scaled action research by teachers and lays out the case for relevant professional development imperative. It closes with a conclusion.

Chapter 4

A Blended Model of Educational Leadership

Effective Leadership Matters

It is generally acknowledged that strong leadership is vital in leveraging school effectiveness. In fact, school effectiveness is inseparable from effective leadership. Leadership is an essential component of school effectiveness. Research suggests that leadership has a substantial influence on organizational performance (Bass & Avolio, 1993; Wasserman et al., 2010). The extent of an individual leader's effect may vary across organizations due to a host of internal and external constraints (Porter & Nohria, 2010). As such, schools that thrive often have leaders who exhibit core leadership skills such as assertiveness, emotional stability, integrity, communication, creativity, delegation, empowerment, and engagement. Extant research links effective leadership to enhanced teaching and learning and overall school effectiveness improvement. In an unobtrusive environment, leadership may significantly affect school culture, leading to organizational performance enhancement. It has direct effects on teaching and learning. Effective leadership is instrumental in improving teaching and learning. Essentially, school leadership is the principal catalyst of school effectiveness.

Leadership has been conceptualized as a change process (Glynn & DeJordy, 2010). Specifically, it has been defined as a "process of social influence" (Prewitt et al., 2011, p. 13), that is, as an interpersonal influence directed toward the achievement of a goal. Barker (2001) believed it is a continuous change process. Mumford et al. (2007) perceived leadership through a *strataplex*, a layered and complex construct consisting of four general categories: cognitive skills, interpersonal skills, business skills, and strategic skills. This view highlights the multi-dimensional basis of leadership.

Furthermore, leadership is also regarded as the formal power and responsibility that a leader holds. In this regard, the leader determines a set of practices or tasks that may increase organizational competitiveness. The leadership of formal, hierarchical leaders is thought to be based on a set of attributes and behaviors (Printy & Marks, 2003). The centrality of leadership in effecting change is emphasized here.

However, measuring leadership effectiveness may be a challenging task. Research has shown that various approaches have been used to measure leadership effectiveness. As the view of school leadership has evolved from an isolated diagnostician or godly decision-maker to a manager sharing responsibilities with others, leadership effectiveness indicators have also changed. Scholars have applied subjective measures such as ratings as well as objective measures such as productivity (Kaiser et al., 2008). Kaiser et al. (2008) suggested two categories of leadership measures to gauge the effectiveness of a leader. The first category focuses on individual leader measures; the second category focuses on groups, teams, and organizations. Overall, improved organizational management and creative innovation are by-products of effective leadership.

The abundance of definitions in the literature is indicative of the elusive and complex nature of leadership. Kaiser et al. (2008) acknowledged the "lack of definitional clarity" (p. 97) of leadership. There is more divergence than convergence regarding the content of leadership. Simply stated, *leadership* is defined here as processes relevant for driving change in an organization. It can be operationalized through enhanced pedagogical competence, professional development (PD) growth, increased individual and collective performance, and other measurable results.

Factors Affecting Effective Leadership

Although leadership is fundamental to organizational success, it can be adversely influenced by subjective factors. Research suggests a congruence of subjective factors may play a significant part in teacher performance reviews and leader-subordinate relationships. These factors, which include early life influences, personal prejudice, and bias, may engender differential teaching effectiveness reviews and in-groups and out-groups. The halo effect, different forms of bias, first impressions effect, in-groups/out-groups, and differing teaching philosophies may interfere with the day-to-day management of a school. Each year, there are reports of biased teacher evaluations, untimely classroom observations, unjustified demotions, unwanted job assignments, devalued contributions, and preferential treatment.

School leaders can distance themselves from teachers when they make statements such as: "I am here for the students. I am not here to be friends with anyone" and "We are not here in the business of spoon-feeding teachers." They may intend to convey a message of no-nonsense leadership. However, their style can help create distance and even mistrust between school leadership and teachers. Needless to say, the words are perceived as a disinvitation to collaborate and cooperate. Teachers are uncomfortable, to say the least. They criticize these administrators for failing to communicate the message, "We are in this together." Instead, the teachers heard, "I am for the kids. You are on your own." Predictably, this leadership style is associated with teacher turnover, job dissatisfaction, burnout, and underperformance. It negatively affects the climate in the workplace. It is worth noting that communication is an integral part of effective leadership.

A leader must be balanced, flexible, adaptable, humble, patient, consistent, reliable, creative, and dependable. An effective leader is a critical thinker, a quick learner, an insightful problem solver, a tireless planner, an ethical and principled innovator, an empathetic strategist, and a team player. It is okay to be aggressive sometimes, but it may not be a good idea to be too aggressive or condescending, especially when communicating with educators.

It is important for a leader to be open to constructive feedback and to show empathy toward subordinates. Lack of empathy can have terrible consequences. A teacher once received an emergency phone call from her daughter's school. Her daughter was very sick and needed urgent care. Before leaving school abruptly, she informed her principal, who apparently approved reluctantly. The following day, the principal did not bother to ask this teacher how her daughter was doing when they crossed paths. The teacher was immensely disturbed by the lack of empathy. Yet, the principal never knew that he had lost that teacher's trust and consideration from that day forward. A principal must attempt to keep up with not only events around school but also major events in employees' lives. This is why being condescending toward employees deprives principals of opportunities to know what their subordinates are going through. No subordinate wants to open up to a patronizing supervisor.

Halo Effect

The halo effect occurs when a positive impression of a subject affects their performance evaluation. Based on likability, attractiveness, or successfulness, this impression has more to do with positive feelings than actual characteristics of the person (J. D. Brown, 1988). Yet, this perception may influence the leader's evaluation of other aspects of the employee's performance. Like any other leaders, school leaders fall prey to this natural inclination, leading to errors in employee performance appraisals. Leaders may even be lenient toward employees' shortcomings (Hynes, 2008). Whereas school leaders might sanction such shortcomings as lack of punctuality, procrastination, missed deadlines, incomplete reports, and absence, they would tend to forgive them if perpetrated by employees they like. Unfortunately, these performance appraisals may not always be documented the same way. Gender bias is another factor that contributes to subjectivity in the appraisal process (Heilman & Haynes, 2008). It has also been reported that teachers treat some students favorably because they perceive the students as being smart, good-mannered, or relatable.

Hawthorne Effect

The Hawthorne effect was introduced by Mayo et al. (J. D. Brown, 1988). The researchers observed that when an observer was present, the production of the workers increased regardless of the conditions that were imposed (J. D. Brown, 1988). For teacher observation, the observer effect can be real, especially if an observation has been announced previously. Some teachers may put on a show, performing above standard when they are observed. They plan thoroughly and deliver an outstanding performance. The classroom dynamics may seem uncharacteristically rehearsed or coached, with teaching aids in place, students participating in a ritualistic manner, and an energized teacher. Conversely, there have been cases when students were passive participants, or the teacher was nervous due to the presence of an observer in the classroom.

Bias

Teachers often complain about a lack of respect, lack of consideration, and lack of support. Some school administrators have garnered an unflattering reputation for treating teachers condescendingly and using teacher evaluations as punishment opportunities. Regarding teachers' evaluations, they are sometimes tinted by evaluators' implicit biases. Berk et al. (2004) examined eight response biases that affect teacher evaluations: (a) halo effect; (b) end-aversion bias; (c) extreme-response bias; (d) acquiescence/yea-saying bias; (e) gender, racial/ethnic, and sexual orientation bias; (f) incompetence bias; (g) buddy bias; and (h) back-scratching bias. These biases may permeate evaluation reports of teacher performance. Mentors, instructional coaches, facilitators, and principals must be aware of their own biases to be able to conduct objective and unbiased evaluations.

In-Group and Out-Group

It is too common that school leaders choose members of these two groups—in-group and out-group—based on trivial or divisive variables such as likability, proximity, perceived common vision, ethnicity, age, attire, gender, sense of humor, sexual orientation, and religion. Such variables may lead to a lack of cohesiveness, which in turn may lead to ineffective or authoritarian managerial practices.

A leader's leadership style is closely associated with the creative work involvement of subordinates. Teachers, administrators, parents, and students have special talents that principals and other educational leaders need to tap into strategically.

The ultimate goal of school leadership should not be individual staff enhancement but collective staff development. Conflicts and ambiguity can be managed effectively if a school leader has the same quality of relationships with all employees. Although this is arguably hard to achieve, school leaders must strive to reach this goal.

Shared Leadership

Researchers have defined *shared leadership* in a variety of ways. Pearce and Conger (2003) defined *shared leadership* as

> A dynamic, interactive influence process among individuals in groups for which the objective is to lead one another to the achievement of group or organizational goals or both. This influence process often involves peer, or lateral, influence and at other times involves upward or downward hierarchical influence (p. 1).

In the context of education, the quality of leader-member exchange (LMX) is vital. Sharing leadership roles with teachers allows teachers to have an influence over, and participate in, school-wide decisions with principals. Louis et al. (2010) noted, "Sharing leadership may have its greatest impact by reducing teacher isolation and increasing commitment to the common good" (p. 41). Any actions that may threaten the hard-won commitment of employees or employee performance must be dealt with accordingly. Chatman and Kennedy (2010) recommended that leaders uphold their commitment to their culture of professionalism and equity even in the most trying times.

The leader's primary job is to empower all subordinates. It is crucial that a school leader identifies a group of employees (key teachers and administrators) with a strong set of skills encompassing professional expertise, procedural knowledge to facilitate professional events, content knowledge, literacy development, technological literacy, curriculum analysis and planning, high ethical standards, credibility, and communication. This group can expand their impact throughout the school. In-group members are expected to take on leadership roles before leading other (out-group) members. Shared leadership is a critical driver of continuous innovation and knowledge creation (Bligh et al., 2006). Shared responsibility is a direct result of leadership delegation. The ultimate outcome of shared or distributed leadership is enhanced organizational performance. The performance of school leadership must be regularly evaluated and reevaluated based on clearly defined performance indicators.

Strategic Leadership

Leaders are expected to demonstrate these leadership skills: extraversion, conscientiousness, emotional stability, agreeableness, rational engagement, openness to experiences, and experiential ability. Clearly, strategic leadership plays a key part in infusing change. The leader is viewed as the principal catalyst of change (Glynn & DeJordy, 2010) or the catalyst of an organization's shared responsibility. Strategic leadership can be approached as "effectuation" (Hitt & Ireland, 2002, p. 10), defined as the process of managing critical resources—social capital and human capital—in order to generate value. The ultimate outcomes of strategic leadership are, in the words of Makri and Scandura (2010), "invention, development, and commercialization" (p. 76). In other words, strategic leadership should result in elevated performance, capital development, and productivity. Kaiser et al. (2008) saw *emergence* and *effectiveness* as metrics for measuring this leadership.

Strategic thinking is key to effective leadership. It requires constant innovation, problem-solving, creativity, transparency, and transformation. It also requires leading organizational change, confronting challenges, confronting identity issues, leading change, stimulating innovation, and handling a diverse group of educators. Adzeh (2017) examined the impact of agreeableness, extraversion, emotional stability, consciousness, rational engagement, openness to experiences, and experiential ability in strategic thinking and noted that extraversion and agreeableness have a more significant influence on leaders' strategic thinking. Essentially, shared leadership is fundamental to the success of an educational organization because it can impact the dynamics and performance of the school.

Conger (2010) described in detail some best practices that are critical for the success of strategic leadership: (a) ensure that a clear strategic framework drives program content and design, (b) ensure that the strategy is translated into corresponding leadership behaviors and mindsets and company capabilities and culture, (c) design the curriculum to elicit group discussions between units and across levels, (d) deploy trained facilitators to provide critical process assistance, (e) cascade the learning experiences down and across multiple levels and operations, and (f) put in place continuous or real-time feedback mechanisms. With regard to feedback, I suggest that each school has an exit interview mechanism for each employee who decides to leave the job. Also, there must be a suggestion box or an electronic platform to collect feedback from employees.

Strategic leadership is often faced with several challenges: insufficient resources, culture issues, motivation issues, communication issues, alignment issues among stakeholders, and resistance to change. Stagnation and status quo also are real perils. Strategic leaders are expected to reflect on the causal factors and explore ways to move forward. Conger (2010) highlighted other problems associated with strategic leadership: poor modeling by leaders, lack of consistent reinforcement, limitations of facilitators, resisting managers blocking the impact of learning, and competing initiatives distracting sponsor support. Although empowerment and autonomy are essential ingredients of strategic leadership, Zhou (2020) contended that excessive autonomy may negatively affect organizational effectiveness. Shoemaker et al. (2013) proposed a framework for evaluating strategic leaders on their ability to anticipate, decide, challenge, interpret, align, and learn. Other challenges include the halo effect, bias, and in-group/out-group.

Chapter 5

Drawing From Other Models of Leadership

Transformational Leadership

Transformational leadership is regarded as an approach that has four key dimensions (Felfe et al., 2004; McLaurin & Al-Amri, 2008; Purvanova & Bono, 2009). The four I's include idealized influence or charisma, inspirational motivation, intellectual motivation, and individualized consideration (Felfe et al., 2004; Judge & Piccolo, 2004). The first dimension of transformational leadership—idealized influence or charisma—is associated with a role model position. The transformational leader provides a clear vision and a sense of mission (Humphreys & Einstein, 2004). To earn the trust and confidence of followers, the leader must exert exceptional moral influence and demonstrate extraordinary performance. As Bass et al. (1987) noted, this is why charismatic leadership is at the heart of the transformational process. The education sector can draw some beneficial elements from transformational leadership.

Transactional Leadership

Akin to transformational leadership, transactional leadership is one of the most studied leadership theories (Judge & Piccolo, 2004). Burns (1978) identified transactional leadership along with transformational leadership in the same study of leadership. Transactional leadership arose from exchange-based theories of the 1980s (Hargis et al., 2011). It is based on rewards and punishments as motivational factors for subordinates. It is worth pointing out that transactional leadership has been used in many organizations, including the information technology field, for over three decades.

Bass et al. (1987) described two motivational factors as *contingent reward,* also known as *constructive transactions* (Antonakis et al., 2003), and *management-by-exception.* Contingent reward leadership places emphasis on rewarding subordinates who meet agreed-upon performance standards (Bass & Avolio, 1993). With regard to management-by-exception, Hargis et al. (2011) identified two types: active management-by-exception and passive management-by-exception. Active management-by-exception is also known as *active corrective transactions* and passive management-by-exception is commonly referred to as *passive corrective transactions* (Antonakis et al., 2003). Generally speaking, there is unequal distribution of contingent rewards and corrective actions. Some transactional leaders tend to err on the side of corrective transactions rather than contingent rewards. The "Carrot Principle" has its benefits (productivity, retention, and engagement). It can also harm intrinsic motivation and employee performance.

The actions of a transactional leader differ from those of a transformational leader. A transactional leader identifies followers' needs and engages in exchange relationships about certain targeted performance objectives (Bass, 1985). Congruent with the transformational leader, the transactional leader's job is to define clear goals and objectives and communicate them to followers. Like the transformational leader, the transactional leader needs to communicate this vision to the followers, enticing acceptance.

The difference lies in the rewards or punishments the followers will bear for meeting or failing to meet expected goals. The rewards can be financial or non-financial. The leader takes corrective action to address behavior concerns (Hargis et al., 2011). While contingent rewards may promote creativity and innovation, it is unclear whether punishments or management-by-exception may augment performance. If allowed to share, rather than oppose, organizational goals, subordinates can have greater influence in decision-making (Vroom & Yetton, 1973). Lowe et al. (1996) found that transformational dimensions and transactional contingent reward are closely correlated. In terms of effectiveness, transformational leadership expands on transactional leadership through an augmentation effect (Ojuola et al., 2020).

Research shows that transformational leadership needs the bargaining power of transactional leadership to communicate a vision. Similarly, transactional leadership leans on transformational leadership to influence followers. The Multifactor Leadership Questionnaire, developed by Bass (1985), has been used to measure certain aspects of the two leadership approaches (Hinkin & Schriesheim, 2008; Schriesheim et al., 2009), including laissez-faire.

Trait Theories

With the changing educational environment, the trait perspective of leadership, also known as the great man theory, seems to be antiquated. It is increasingly inconceivable that a single leader—a great man or great woman—decides the destiny of an organization. Social organizations evolve. Traits that were once useful may not be suitable in today's modern environment (Van Vugt et al., 2008). The notion of a born, great school leader makes little sense today.

Research has suggested that leadership can be genetic (Judge et al., 2009). Such traits as personality, intelligence, attractiveness, and height can be associated with genes. Leaders who exhibit these traits are thought to have genetic predispositions. The extent to which genetics predisposes one to a leadership position is debatable. However, it is increasingly argued that an effective leader needs more than inherited psychological and physical characteristics to be able to unlock the hidden potential of subordinates.

Despite the apparent fall of the trait perspective of leadership, leaders can still draw upon some of the traits to lead their subordinates. The study of the Big Five traits revealed that traits can correlate positively or negatively with leadership emergence and effectiveness. Judge et al. (2009) argued that bright personality traits, which include extraversion, agreeableness, conscientiousness, emotional stability, core self-evaluations, intelligence, charisma, and openness to experience, may prove to be extremely useful for a leader to have. These traits are said to be constructive for leadership. Because leaders must communicate a compelling vision to subordinates and must infuse meaningful change, these characteristics have an essential part to play. The authors also explored dark traits that may be destructive for a leader. These traits—narcissism, hubris, social dominance, and Machiavellianism—may negatively affect a leader. Taken together, bright and dark traits cannot account fully for the emergence and exercise of effective leadership, especially in the information technology world.

Many studies have identified other traits related to leadership. Of all the traits found in the literature, two—integrity (Palanski & Yammarino, 2009) and wakefulness (Marques, 2006)—are worth mentioning. Research has shown that integrity is positively associated with a leader's performance. Not only can the integrity of a leader influence the job performance of subordinates, as Palanski and Yammarino (2009) observed, but it can also influence a subordinate to have integrity. On the other hand, wakefulness is said to be an important element of effective leadership (Marques, 2006). Ultimately, the strategic importance of integrity and wakefulness is unquestionable.

A heightened understanding of the innate qualities or attributes of educational professionals—extroversion vs. introversion, sensing vs. intuition, thinking vs. feeling, and judging vs. perceiving—may make a difference. Therefore, a leader must assume more than one role. Maccoby (1996) suggested eight roles, four of which stand out: innovator, facilitator, mentor, and coordinator. These roles are fundamental to the exercise of leadership. Trait theories are not baseless. Although scholars tend to move away from trait theories and focus on other leadership theories, such as behavioral, contingency, and relational theories, personality traits should still be examined for what they are worth. Ignoring leaders' traits may have deleterious consequences.

Leader-Member Exchange Theory

The failure of school improvement plans has been linked to a lack of leadership. Effective leaders are known to capitalize on personal development, collective effort, and employee commitment. The salience of LMX theory rests on the premise that the quality of leader–employee relationships may harness beneficial effects for an organization (Uhl-Bien, 2006). Research shows that LMX, as a dyadic relationship, is tied to performance outcomes. LMX is reported to influence job performance, job satisfaction, citizenship behaviors, and organizational commitment (Walumbwa et al., 2010). The LMX theory appears to be a suitable vehicle for enhancing educational leadership and, subsequently, school effectiveness.

The LMX theory contends that leaders establish different types of relationships with each of their subordinates (Greguras & Ford, 2006). Leaders form two groups of subordinates: in-group and out-group. While the in-group comprises protégés who enjoy special treatment—such as special promotions and assignments, career advancement opportunities, and special recognitions—the out-group is almost ostracized, given less attention and fewer acknowledgments (Lunenburg, 2010). Sometimes, they receive the professional respect that out-group members do not enjoy. In doing so, leaders may undermine their own power and effectiveness.

Rather than engaging in high-quality relationships—also referred to as *high LMX*—with the in-group and low-quality relationships—commonly known as *low LMX*—with the out-group, a leader should appropriately utilize LMX as an empowerment and professional culture-building tool for constructing rich rapport with all employees equally. Should leaders adopt the high and low LMX stance, they must strike the right balance between high LMX and low LMX. In their study of the link between ethical leadership and LMX, Walumbwa et al. (2010) noted that the improvement of employee performance can be achieved through, among other factors, high-quality LMX and identification with the organization.

The expected outcomes of leadership, according to McLaurin and Al-Amri (2008), are technical development and a higher level of motivation. Indeed, these goals are inherent in the LMX theory. LMX has similar positive outcomes, such as job enrichment, job satisfaction, job performance, organizational commitment, and citizenship behaviors (DeConinck, 2009). This is especially true about the relationships between the leader and the in-group, characterized by liking, respect, and mutual trust (DeConinck, 2009). Lunenburg (2010) argued that the in-group members are often given more job responsibility and more favorable performance ratings. The consequences of differentiated treatment of employees may vary. The stress of in-group members is believed to originate from added responsibilities, whereas the stress of out-group members is said to emanate from exclusion.

Conversely, there may also be a link, however weak, between LMX and job turnover intentions and burnout. Discussing the importance of the dynamics of LMX, Borchgrevink and Boster (1997) observed that low LMX between the leader and the out-group may negatively impact employee burnout, job turnover, job satisfaction, job performance, organizational climate, and organizational commitment. Tepper (2000) claimed that leaders' condescending and unfair attitudes may alienate and demoralize followers. It should be noted that the quality of LMX relationships affects followers' attitudes and performance in different ways.

Conclusion

Drawing positive elements from different leadership theories may bear significant promise. It has been established that educational professionals have some unique characteristics. However, it takes shared leadership, creative leadership, flexible leadership, and strategic leadership to unleash their untapped creative power. I suggest a model of educational leadership that integrates LMX with other forms of leadership. My idea is that high-quality exchanges between team members and leaders enhance innovative and creative behavior in a K–12 context. Such exchanges improve organizational performance and increase accountability. Lack of effective leadership has been found to be one of the causal factors of failed projects and ineffective educational practices. Undoubtedly, traditional leadership perspectives have limited effectiveness in today's highly competitive educational environment. Bligh et al. (2006) contended that shared leadership can drive and enable continuous innovation, knowledge creation, and productivity. There are conflicting reports about the link between LMX and innovativeness (Lee, 2008). However, studies have found that both shared leadership and LMX can lower the stress levels of leaders and subordinates. Hence, blending the different approaches appears to be a step in the right direction, especially in the globalization context. School leaders must be visionaries with broad-based skills.

> Today's principal must be a legal expert, health and social services coordinator, fundraiser, public relations consultant, parental involvement expert, and security expert, who is technologically savvy, diplomatic, with top-notch managerial skills, whose most important duty is the implementation of instructional programs, curricula, pedagogical practice, and assessment models (Schiff, 2001, p. 1).

I would dare to add that principals must be able to imagine new realities and set their sights on new heights and new possibilities. They should take time to celebrate their accomplishments, however small or big. However, they should not be lured into a false sense of self-importance. If anything, they should learn from their successes as seeds for other possibilities. It is all about teamwork. Moreover, they must also understand, however vaguely, different contours of new technologies, including artificial intelligence, and how they might impact students' lives.

Chapter 6

Improving Instruction Quality and Managing Diversity

Introduction

Teachers often receive the lion's share of the blame for students' academic failure. They are regarded as the most important resource in student success. Research suggests that effective teaching fuels elevated student performance. A considerable body of evidence supports the argument that the quality of instruction is positively correlated with learning outcomes (Breaux & Wong, 2003; Jenkins, 2003). While the teacher plays a critical role in driving student achievement, effective teaching is not the only driver of student success. Several factors affect student learning. Louis et al. (2010) postulated that student achievement is linked to the combined influence of work settings, capacity, motivation, and collective leadership.

Clearly, a host of contributing factors are responsible for student academic attainment. They include student factors (characteristics, motivation, intellectual ability, and language), family and home factors (socioeconomic status, parental involvement/support, and educational background), school factors (organizational culture, leadership, academic practices, conditions, instructional programs, resources, and personnel support/development), peer factors (beliefs, aspirations, values, goals, and education), and teacher factors (experience, qualification, expertise, pedagogical preparation, and commitment). Unless all these factors are in sync, students may not achieve their optimal learning potential. Any of these factors can enhance or lower student performance. For example, peer pressure, home structure, work conditions, and parental involvement can exert direct positive or negative effects on student achievement.

Granted, parents can be very busy. They cannot make it to all meetings at their child's school. Fortunately, there are many ways for a parent to stay connected with a school today: text message, telephone, email, mailing lists, discussion boards, course management systems, social media, and instant messaging. Most parents and guardians have cell phones that can allow for e-communication with the school and to check a child's grades and behavior through student information systems such as PowerSchool. This can make a tremendous difference in the child's performance at school. It is unfortunate that some parents never communicate with their child's school, and some only show up when there is a major problem at school.

With respect to student factors, it is important that students comprehend the true value of educational empowerment. Education is the gateway to a broad range of opportunities from college to employment. To counter this argument, some students often point out that some prominent entrepreneurs such as Mark Zuckerberg of Facebook, Bill Gates of Microsoft, Steve Jobs of Apple, and Michael Dell of Dell Computer are all college dropouts. It is worth noting that these entrepreneurs must have been academically gifted to be able to think outside of the box and fill a void. In fact, there is a scarcity of such creative entrepreneurs today.

Despite ample evidence that suggests that education prepares individuals for their whole lives, educators still have the daunting task of explaining to students that education is their gateway to college, careers, and civic life. The quality of courses taken, grades earned, books read, knowledge and experiences accumulated, and commitment demonstrated may be the difference between poverty and career success.

I am often astounded to hear students brag about not studying before a test, not caring about courses, deliberately skipping classes, not reading books, and so forth. "I never study before a test." "I don't care about that class." "I did not study before I took the SAT exam." These are statements I have heard from students. Yet, research findings continue to show a link between studying and student academic performance. In some countries, such as India, South Korea, and the Democratic Republic of the Congo, college admission depends on the student's success in national exams. For example, I was one of 14 students out of 35 who passed the national exam in my native school back home. That year, 21 of my classmates failed the national exam and had to retake it the following year. A few of them never graduated from high school because they failed the national exam more than once. Passing the national exam is a major graduation requirement in the Democratic Republic of the Congo. My classmates and I spent days preparing for the exam in small study groups. We studied night and day. In the United States, there is no national exam requirement for graduation. While there are course credit requirements, students do not deal with the pressure of passing a standardized national exam.

Students should shoulder their responsibility for their academic performance. One student, a 10th grader, laid the blame for student academic failure on students. He said,

> Most of the time, if a student is struggling or is not performing academically, it is the student's fault. You did not take the initiative to better yourself. There is not such a thing as a lack of knowledge; there is a lack of trying. The true secret to academic success is initial development by the parents. Spending time with their child to help them, and maybe even themselves, learn at a young age. The teacher must then utilize the skills the child already has by integrating them into a collaborative learning environment.

He suggested that parents, students, and teachers need to work in tandem. Parents' early involvement in developing learning predisposition plays a significant part in a child's intellectual growth. Teachers should capitalize on what the parents have sowed, and the student needs to take control of the learning process by studying, asking questions, and seeking help.

Drivers of Student Learning

Considerable research has discussed enablers and inhibitors of student learning. However, I thought it worthwhile that educators hear directly from high school students. So, what do students think about drivers and inhibitors of student learning? Several high school students shared their views on ways to improve teacher effectiveness. Following are their statements taken from a video (https://www.youtube.com/watch?v=T7QtJXdZxMU).

"I learn best when..."

1. "The teacher makes the class interactive and fun; he or she is not simply lecturing or giving students notes and expecting students to complete worksheets."
2. "The teacher uses hands-on activities."

3. "The teacher challenges us."
4. "The teacher uses visual representations or visual aids."
5. "The teacher interacts with us, and the class behaves."
6. "The teacher has control of the class."
7. "The teacher gives us tutorials."
8. "I interact with other students and complete hands-on activities."
9. "I build something, break things down."
10. "We have Socratic seminars."
11. "The teacher structures activities from simple to complex."
12. "I know exactly what we are doing, and there is some form of formality; we don't call people by their nicknames."
13. "The teacher explains things in detail."
14. "The teacher lets us interact with other classmates."
15. "The class behaves."
16. "The teacher pushes and motivates me."
17. "The teacher connects what we are learning to real-life things."
18. "Things explode."
19. "The teacher organizes topics from easiest to hardest."
20. "The teacher has a good structure of the materials that we will be covering."
21. "I know exactly what we are going to be doing."
22. "The teacher gives examples."
23. "The teacher gives good notes."

"I feel challenged when..."

1. "The teacher asks about my philosophy and connects what we are doing to my life."
2. "The teacher encourages me and pushes me to think outside of the box and encourages me to form my own opinion and make decisions about certain issues."

3. “The teacher encourages me to apply what I am learning in real life.”
4. “The teacher gives me independent tasks to complete.”
5. “The teacher holds open forums and Socratic seminars to discuss and debate different topics. I like it when the teacher lets everyone express their opinions.”
6. “The teacher has office hours, and during office hours, they actually help you instead of letting you figure it out by yourself.”
7. “The teacher has a clear idea about what he or she is trying to teach.”
8. “The teacher goes over information and relates it to real life so that whenever we have a test or a quiz, we can relate back to the story the teacher told us. This can only work for certain classes like history maybe biology. For math, I like it when the teacher goes over several examples and goes step-by-step because many students need steps to understand a problem.”
9. “The teacher shares their own experiences.”
10. “The teacher relates the lesson to real life.”
11. “The teacher encourages me inside and outside of the classroom.”
12. “The teacher asks me what I need instead of assuming what I need to learn in class.”
13. “The teacher makes the classroom an interesting environment and makes it a serious environment when necessary, but not all the time.”
14. “The teacher goes over test questions that I did not understand.”
15. “The teacher involves us, interacts with us, gets us in a group, and makes us move around.”
16. “My teacher pushes me to learn instead of letting me fall behind.”

17. "My teacher talks about positive things instead of negative things."
18. "The teacher has fun with the learning."
19. "The teacher interacts with students rather than giving bookwork."
20. "My teacher gives good notes, knows what he or she is talking about, and can explain to me when I have a question; and has an interesting class: we play games and have interactive notes or something to keep the class interesting, keeps the class under control."
21. "The teacher gives us a problem, puts us in groups, and asks us to solve the problems."
22. "My teacher breaks down a concept to my understanding."
23. "My teacher takes the time to make sure I understand the lesson before moving on to the next lesson."

"I can be successful when..."

1. "My teacher interacts with us on a one-on-one basis."
2. "The class is small, and the teacher goes over things several times instead of just one time."
3. "My teacher and I have a good relationship; the teacher puts in extra time to make sure I master the material."
4. "My teacher and I get along very well and can collaborate."
5. "The teacher establishes order. For example, class is not to be taken lightly, work must be turned in on time, they don't like talking, they will take your phone, or you need to be on time; they have clear procedures in place about tardiness and makeup work. Success equals order."
6. "I have a good classroom environment, and my teacher has clear expectations for students."
7. "My teacher encourages me to study."

8. "I am challenged by my teacher and other students in the class when we work together, and when I have a great learning environment; if I don't know an answer, other students can help; we help one another."
9. "I listen to my teacher and have a positive attitude."

Inhibitors of Student Learning

In the same video, students also offered their opinions about inhibitors that impede their abilities to learn effectively. The following are statements from the same students.

"I have trouble in my class when..."

1. "My teacher teaches stuff students won't need in their future."
2. "My teacher is obsessed with grades and tests."
3. "The teacher only lectures without class participation or in-between activities."
4. "I don't come to school, fail to get my work done, or let other students influence me."
5. "Other students make noise."
6. "Things are not organized, and the teacher does not know what he or she is trying to do and is always angry."
7. "The teacher gives notes and is not able to fully explain the notes."
8. "The teacher does not stay after school or does not make time for extra help."
9. "The teacher assigns a project, does not fully explain it, or shows an example of the project."
10. "Someone is always distracting me, trying to get me off task, unfocused."

11. "I disrespect my teacher, talk back, or talk to classmates."
12. "My teacher teaches a brief lesson and does not go in depth."
13. "My teacher is mad, shuts up, and sits in his or her own corner."
14. "My teacher is redundant."
15. "Common Core is retarded."
16. "Obsession with tests and grades take the fun out of learning."
17. "The fun of learning is missing."
18. "It is impossible to have a fully engaged student."

Students recorded this video in 2011 when Common Core was being implemented. However, the content is still relevant today. Students cited teachers' mastery of the course content, class structure, nature of interactions, modeling, real-life connection, classroom management, student autonomy and independence, learning styles, challenges, and visual aids as some of the drivers of student learning. On the other hand, teachers' obsession with tests, long lectures, lack of organization and discipline, and absence of fun were mentioned as inhibitors of student learning.

Knowing Students

American schools reflect the basic values that make up the hallmark of American culture. Those values include (but are not limited to) equality of opportunity, individual freedom, independence, individualism, democracy, competition, justice, human rights, directness, informality, and success. Essentially, they affect the classroom dynamic and the classroom environment. American students are fully aware that their individual rights are protected. They will confront and oppose authoritarian or tyrannical styles of teaching.

They will not blindly follow a teacher-prescribed agenda. The basic tenet of any teaching philosophy in this country is that teaching is an act of creation and cocreation. Thus, a teacher is regarded as a facilitator of the learning process, a guide on the side, a helper, and a mentor. There is general consensus here that a student is not an empty vessel to be filled, and a teacher is not a figure of unquestionable authority or knowledge, a sage on the stage, or the fountain of knowledge. In short, a teacher is not regarded as a know-it-all and should not act as one.

An African teacher once described his role as a teacher as follows: "A teacher is like a father; you respect him; you believe in him; then, you can begin to learn." This view is in stark contrast to how some American students perceive their teachers. It is not shared by many American students who are quick to remind a teacher, "Don't yell at me. You are not my father. We have the freedom of speech in this country."

I once asked an American student who was being rude to me to talk to me the way he would talk to his own father. His response shocked me: "You don't want me to talk to you the way I talk to my father. I don't like my father. If you think I am being rude now, you should hear me talk to my father." I did not expect that response! The relationship I had with my father before he passed away was not the same as what my American student had with his father. My idea of a father figure was not in alignment with his. He described his father as a "deadbeat dad" who was not in his life. We had different upbringings and different perceptions of father figures! My parents were devoted Catholics who raised eight children and remained married until my father passed away.

While stern disciplinarians may be feared in some undemocratic countries where authoritarianism still prevails, this does not seem to be the case in the United States. Teachers earn respect and credibility through hard work, work ethic, relationship building, and skillful teaching. Teachers should respect each student's individuality and should teach democratically. In the United States, teachers are expected to treat all students equally and impartially. Any perceived favoritism or bribery can be costly. Openness, fairness, credibility, empathy, objectivity, strong work ethic, and preparedness can earn a teacher's respect and trust. Students will hold the teacher accountable. In some countries, for example, teachers rarely discuss their agendas, the teacher's teaching style, the grading criteria, the content taught, and the teacher's approach to classroom management. Student feedback is perceived as a negative challenge, a threat to the teacher's authority.

There is a huge gap between educators and learners. In the United States, students will ask questions about various aspects of the class: their grades, the length of the presentation, the teacher's teaching style, questioning style, foreign accent, personalized feedback, attire, and personal life. Some of these questions may be embarrassing. Teachers should expect to face misunderstandings due to language, nonverbal communication, arguments about sensitive topics, etc. Subsequently, cultural differences and cultural clashes are bound to create a certain degree of discomfort and discord. Culture shock may arise as a result of students' misbehaviors, such as talking back, acting out to gain attention, showing hostility, ignoring class rules, moving about without permission, leaving the classroom without permission, tardiness, and so forth. Teachers should face these challenges with patience and open-mindedness. Students act out for a variety of reasons: to seek assistance, to express frustration over the teaching approach, the agenda, and learning activities, or to gain attention.

Understanding the language, the vernacular, the experiences, the aspirations, and the values of students can lead to a successful teaching career and can help minimize the culture gap. In the early months of my teaching career in an American public school, I was unaware of many things my students talked passionately about. Hence, I felt compelled to watch TV programs on MTV, BET, TV One, truTV, and other networks and to listen to some of my students' favorite radio programs just to acquaint myself with their experiences.

This was particularly rewarding because students were genuinely pleased to discuss with me some of their favorite radio and TV programs. As a devoted fan of the National Basketball Association, I remember discussing the outcomes of some playoff games with my students, who were mildly impressed with my knowledge of the players. I read certain books that my students recommended. One example is *The Pact: Three Young Men Make a Promise and Fulfill a Dream* by Lisa Frazier Page, Sampson Davis, Rameck Hunt, and George Jenkins. I watched certain movies that my students suggested. The last one was "When They See Us" on Netflix. As a result, I developed closer connections with my students. A teacher from Jamaica had a Skype-mediated video conference connecting her American students with Jamaican students. Students from both countries shared their experiences about the computer hardware and software they use. It was a very positive experience for all involved.

In today's technologically driven world, teachers should help students take virtual tours. With Google Earth, I once gave my students a virtual tour of my native country. They were pleasantly surprised to see certain things they did not expect, such as roads, buildings, churches, etc. Undoubtedly, the closer a teacher is to his or her students, the more effective he or she becomes as an educator. Subsequently, the communication gap will decrease, and so will discipline problems.

Marzano (2017) provided specific strategies about relationship building that can assist teachers: greeting students at the classroom door, holding informal conferences, attending after-school functions, giving students special responsibilities or leadership roles in the classroom, scheduling interaction, creating a photo bulletin board, and using humor. To understand students' backgrounds and interests, Marzano further provided strategies to help teachers gather students' background information and interests:

1. student background surveys;
2. opinion questionnaires;
3. individual teacher-student conferences;
4. the school newspaper, newsletter, or bulletin;
5. informal class interviews;
6. familiarity with student culture;
7. autobiographical metaphors and analogies;
8. six-word autobiographies;
9. independent investigations;
10. quotes;
11. comments about student achievement or areas of importance;
12. lineups; and
13. individual student learning goals.

These strategies are worth investigating and implementing. It is not enough to know students. Students need structure and value-added instruction to perform to the best of their abilities.

What is true for teachers also applies to school leaders. They have a duty to know by name as many faculty members and as many students as possible. I have been very impressed by the unique way the principal of one of the high schools involved in the study learns his faculty members' names and is able to connect faces with names in a very short period of time.

The key to classroom management is training in effective classroom management techniques. Being deeply knowledgeable about course content is not enough. The teacher should know how to run a classroom and bridge the cultural divide without being overbearing! This means it is vital to know your students. One of the first projects my students regularly completed was a multimedia product focused on self-introduction: their educational experiences, their course expectations, their career goals, their hobbies and interests, their values, their dream jobs, their dream houses, their favorite teachers, their worst teachers, their learning styles, their favorite songs, their favorite movie stars, and so forth. I asked them to present the project to the class. Students took personal gratification in sharing their getting-to-know-you projects. If you know your students, not just their names, you can anticipate potential discipline problems. You will also learn what may lead to student boredom or to active student engagement. A solid teacher preparation program is the first step, followed by an effective, continuous development program. Learning from other instructional leaders—an instructional coach, a mentor, a facilitator, and peers—is supremely important. Finally, school districts should plan to integrate cultural sensitization of immigrant teachers into a new faculty orientation program. Many school districts lack cultural sensitization programs to introduce immigrant teachers to the culture of this country.

Immigrant teachers, especially minority immigrant teachers, may also experience some instances of microaggressions (Sissoko & Nadal, 2021). Students sometimes find it amusing to make fun of their immigrant teachers' accents. I have seen this countless times. Unfortunately, even some teachers think it is harmless and funny to mimic their foreign-born colleagues' accents in their presence. It is not unusual to see teachers speak for or explain to foreign-born teachers as if they need help. Sometimes, they oversimplify the language or slow down the language, bordering on infantilization. Other types of microaggressions they may experience include underestimation of content knowledge, devaluation of technical ability, and insensitive or sarcastic remarks. They may also expect to be treated differently. A foreign-born teacher once called a parent to discuss a discipline concern. The parent ended the conversation hastily and abruptly: "I am not going to sit here trying to figure out what you are trying to say. Good-bye." Instead of being upset, here is an opportunity to take things in stride with a good dose of humor.

I recommend that immigrant teachers learn to cope with these microaggressions with a sense of humor. What is true is that their skills and presence are valued once they show that they are adequately qualified for the job. On the flip side, many students and teachers are often genuinely appreciative of the skill set and diversity that immigrant teachers bring to the table. Some probe about their cultures, foods, and languages. Many students do not care where their teachers come from as long as they are qualified and do not have a negative impact on their education.

Surveys play an important role in teaching. I recommend that teachers have students complete learning style surveys at the beginning of the semester. Several web-based learning style surveys are available online for teachers to choose from. These surveys can help teachers learn a great deal about students' learning preferences. On the other hand, Brookfield's (2006) Critical Incident Questionnaire (CIQ) is an excellent resource for post-activity or post-assessment feedback. It helps teachers explore students' reactions to teaching practicum, reflect on teaching practices, and subsequently adjust instructional strategies. As Brookfield (1995) noted, the CIQ allows teachers to capture "vivid happenings" (p. 114) that occur in the classroom. Essentially, the CIQ is about actions or events that cause students to be engaged, distant, confused, surprised, puzzled, or irritated. It encourages students to reflect on the teaching process. Teachers are encouraged to design their own modified version of the CIQ and have students complete it online.

Knowing students also entails being aware of their needs. Maslow (1970) hierarchically listed students' needs as follows: physiological needs, safety needs, love and belonging needs, esteem needs, and self-actualization needs, as presented in Figure 7.

Figure 7. Maslow's Hierarchy of Needs

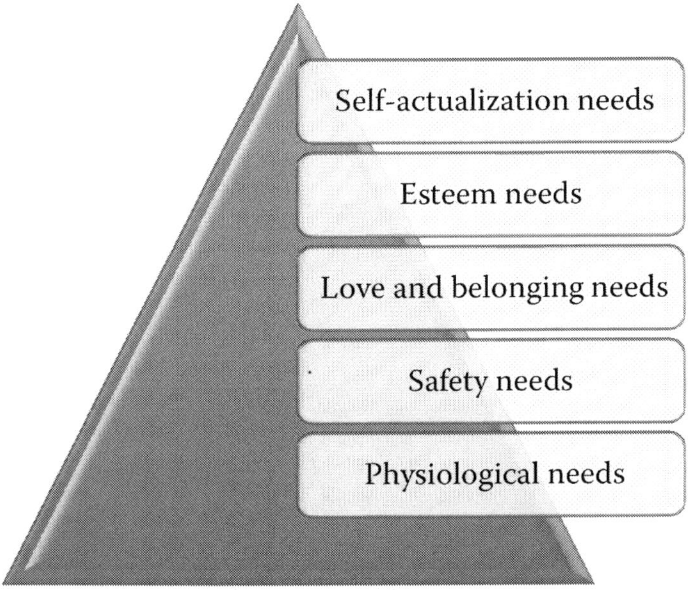

It is the societal responsibility to ensure that basic needs are attended to. Students may lose their sense of self-confidence and self-worth in a classroom that does not provide much-needed safety, support, and protection.

Overcoming Obstacles

There are several reports of immigrant teachers quitting after a short period of time. Some of the complaints I have heard from students over the years include:

"We don't like the way he talks to us."

"I don't like his tone of voice."

"He can't teach."

"I need my personal space. He gets too close."

"She thinks she is better than us."

"She does not like Black kids."

"She thinks we are stupid!"

"He is often unprepared and disorganized."

"He does not understand American students."

"She does not know how to teach or how to relate to American kids."

"He is different. He is not like us."

"He does not teach like American teachers."

"He does not grade our assignments correctly! He gives fake grades."

"I cannot understand him; he has an accent."

Naturally, immigrant teachers should expect to encounter some resistance in the U.S. classroom. When trouble arises, it is important that they seek advice from experienced teachers and school administrators. They should refrain from losing their temper. There have been cases of immigrant teachers taking refuge in their native language to vent their frustration. That is a professional blunder. With all the digital voice-recording devices available, students can easily record your words and translate them into English instantly. It is safer to address the issue at hand in a non-confrontational manner. Some immigrant teachers opt to engage in verbal arguments with students. That, also, is a mistake. A verbal argument may escalate into an unexpected physical confrontation. When a student has an audience, anything can happen. Some teachers resolve to quit over their inability to teach or to relate with American students. Quitting over challenges should not be an option if you really love teaching.

Challenges should contribute to professional growth. Challenge avoidance can hurt one's chances of becoming an effective teacher. It is important to recognize the patterns of the negative behaviors that take place in your class and to anticipate minor and major misbehaviors before they occur. When they do occur, you must know how to strategically and pragmatically address them in a non-confrontational manner with a peaceful resolution as an ultimate outcome. Teachers must arm themselves with a variety of de-escalation strategies to deal with discipline problems and to defuse tension or any lingering misunderstanding. Students' trust will derive from students' appreciation of the teacher's knowledge/expertise, of the teacher's ability to teach, and of the teacher's respect for students. Students seem to have little to no tolerance for public humiliation, disrespect, devaluing of their intelligence, and condescending attitudes.

With respect to licensure requirements, it is important to know what type of licenses you need to teach in the United States. There are several types of licenses—initial license, standard or professional license, special license, conditional or emergency license—and endorsements. Furthermore, prospective teachers must find out the licensure requirements: What PRAXIS assessment and what program of study, if any, best suits them? What college offers courses required for teaching certification? Another consideration is the evaluation of international education. Finally, it helps to inquire about tenure requirements early on.

Immigrant teachers must take the time to familiarize themselves with the tenets of American education. According to the USDE, the principles guiding American education include climate and prevention, clear, appropriate, and consistent expectations and consequences, and equity and continuous improvement (Duncan, 2014). Teachers are encouraged to foster a positive classroom climate that equitably prevents problem behaviors, sets high expectations, and drives achievement and engagement for all students to thrive. As Chickering (2006) observed, communicating high expectations and respecting diverse talents and ways of learning are essential for student academic achievement. L. Kim (2004) suggested three ways of communicating high expectations: giving challenging assignments, providing examples or models for students to follow, and publicly praising exemplary work.

Furthermore, it is important that immigrant teachers join professional learning communities (PLCs), discussion groups, and educators' professional organizations. They are encouraged to subscribe to good blogs and good journals about teaching to get updates on research, resources, and instructional strategies that can assist them. They should also seek support from experienced colleagues. In fact, PD opportunities contribute to strengthening some good teaching practices and to correcting some weaknesses. Content planning sessions, department meetings, and PD activities provide rewarding learning opportunities. Additionally, district-sponsored curriculum alignment meetings, state-sponsored summer training workshops, school-based content planning sessions, and teacher-to-teacher experience-sharing sessions help reveal a variety of new resources as well as new teaching strategies.

Teacher Talk: A Gateway to Student Language Fossilization

One of the problems confronting English language learners (ELLs) in K–12 education is the potential for fossilization. Coined by Selinker (1972), *fossilization* is defined as a failure for second language (L2) learners to reach target-level language proficiency (Combs, 2009). There are various forms of fossilization: phonological, morphological, syntactic, semantic, and pragmatic. According to the Selective Fossilization Hypothesis, one source of fossilization is the interaction between first language (L1) transfer and the attributes of L2 input (Han, 2013). Other known causal factors include language transfer, training transfer, learning strategy, communication strategy, and overgeneralization (Wei, 2008). The potential for language fossilization looms large in K–12 classrooms.

Teacher talk is the language of instruction used by teachers in their interactions with students. The form and content of that language may significantly impact a student's language output. Surprisingly, not many studies exist on the effects of teacher talk on learners' fossilization. While teacher talk has the power to guide learners to develop standard language proficiency, it also adversely affects student language growth. The form and content of teacher talk may significantly impact a student's language output. L1 proficiency development is dependent on formal language instruction. Lack thereof may partly account for student fossilized language.

Essentially, the quality of teacher talk is vital. It provides students with the critical, comprehensible input they need for language development. Stephen Krashen's Input Hypothesis postulates that "the mental mechanisms of language learning are driven mainly by the learner's experience of comprehensible input, that is, messages expressed at an appropriate level of linguistic complexity and in a helpful context" (Lynch, 1996, pp. 13–14). Hence, teachers' proper use of the target language drives and influences students to learn it. Such a discourse can help students, especially ELLs, develop English language proficiency. Ultimately, there is value for teachers in adopting appropriate academic discourse around students. Teachers should constantly monitor what they say around students and how they say it.

Learner Interpretation: Confirmation

Indeed, teacher talk plays a significant part in the learner's language fossilization. It can be assumed that the teacher's use of a vernacular, casual version of English in the classroom has a fossilization effect on student language, especially for ELLs with limited English proficiency. Students who hear such constructions as "I should have went," "I should have did it yesterday," "I should have came," "We was," "He had wrote that letter," "He is asking all them questions," "He don't know," "Who do you think you is," "He had came," and "It don't matter" from a teacher (especially, an English teacher) may begin to think of them as grammatically correct constructions. This may lead to syntactic fossilization. Rather than addressing instances of incorrectness with corrective feedback, the teacher becomes a vector of fossilization because of the strong possibility of fossilization as a result. Similarly, a student who hears such pronouns as "hisself" and "theirself" may never question their grammatical correctness and will internalize these natural mistakes, leading to morphological fossilization. In other words, fossilization is reinforced by teacher talk because students will interpret those deviancies as confirmation of the correctness of those structures. "My teacher also says it" is the metamessage. Students will be misled into considering the abovementioned deviancies as correct language use because they are uttered by teachers whom they look up to.

Risk of Fossilization Among Native Speakers

Fossilization is not limited to nonnative speakers. As native speakers move from the natural language to English for Academic Purposes (EAP), the transition primarily needs support from teachers. EAP learning requires a good amount of metacognition. Students should be taught to think about the linguistic structures governing the language. The centrality of the teacher's guiding role is more than crucial. Let's examine the two examples below:

Example 1:

I once tried to correct a female African-American student in an honors Scientific and Technical Visualization class. The student said, "He did it hisself."

I corrected her: "'Himself'" not 'hisself.'"

Unfortunately, she was convinced that I was wrong. "I always say 'hisself.'" She rejected my suggestion. "I have been saying this my entire life and no one has ever told me it was wrong," she said. "My parents, my teachers, no one has ever said anything about it. You were not even born in this country. . . . How can you correct my English?" she asked.

She was supported by one of her classmates, a mixed-race male student. "Don't listen to him. You are right and he is wrong. He is not even a native speaker of English. This is not an English class and he is not your English teacher," he said in a matter-of-fact tone of voice.

I reminded the two students that I was a licensed English as a Second Language (ESL) teacher, in addition to my technology education licenses.

The young lady adamantly believed that her rationale made sense: "We say 'herself' for 'her,' 'theirself' for 'their,' and 'hisself' for 'his.'"

After a relatively short discussion, I asked the student to review the use of personal pronouns online. I suggested an educational web link about personal pronouns. After reviewing multiple resources—not trusting my suggested resource—about the correct grammatical use of personal pronouns, the young lady admitted that she was wrong and accepted my correction.

"How come nobody has ever corrected me? You are the first teacher to tell me this just before I graduate from high school."

As can be seen, native speakers may also fall victim to fossilized language if not checked. Without giving any thought to it, the pronoun "hisself" has become fossilized within her natural language.

Example 2:

A student was several minutes late to class. She found her classmates working on a project she was not fond of. She exclaimed loudly, "I should not have came to this class today!"

The teacher explained to the student that the project was rather interesting and challenging. The teacher also seized the opportunity to correct the student's grammatical error. Approaching the student, the teacher suggested softly, making sure the rest of the class did not hear, "By the way, I should have come," the teacher offered a correction.

The student was angered by the correction. Almost shouting, she said, "Don't worry about my language. I speak the way I want to speak. I don't care about what people may think about the way I talk."

The teacher further encouraged the student to watch how she speaks because she was just a few weeks away from her high school graduation. "In 4 weeks, the school will be over and you will be graduating. Soon you will be a college student. I am sure you are planning to go to college."

Interrupting abruptly, the student said, "Of course, I am going to college."

The teacher continued, "Then, it is important that you pay special attention to your grammar."

The student was angered by the teacher's attention to her English. "You are making me so mad. I speak the way I want to speak. Don't worry about how I talk. I know how to switch from casual English to formal English. Besides, everyone I know speaks like this." she said angrily.

Like this student, many students argue that they know when and how to code-switch. They claim that they know when not to use the colloquial, conversational English they use with their peers and switch to a more standard version of English in formal circumstances such as job interviews and college. Teachers should emphasize that success in college or in a job also depends on a good command of standard EAP. All teachers must invariably play a role in students' EAP and literacy growth. Students must be trained in effective communication skills.

Pedagogical Responsibility of Teachers

When interacting with students, teachers must heighten their vocabulary and demonstrate good command of the English language by employing a high level of grammatical correctness and eloquence. Students aspire to target academic language mastery. Teachers have a pedagogical obligation to expose students to grammatically sound written or verbal language at school. The way teachers speak about students matters significantly. The "what to" and "how to" of teacher talk have a direct or indirect effect on student academic language mastery. Teachers should maintain a high level of language proficiency and fluency at all times. They are expected to model effective language skills—reading, listening, writing, and speaking. It is disconcerting to note that some teachers do not always expose students to high levels of EAP to prepare them for college and employment. In fact, it is not uncommon to see teachers employ the same conversational vernacular with students that students use during social or academic interactions. Teachers' structural language deviancy reinforces learners' language errors, which may ultimately lead to student fragmented language growth—temporarily or permanently. It is crucial that teachers use grammatically correct, academic English around students.

School leadership should set standards for positive communication. The way teachers communicate with and around students is extremely important. Specifically, teacher talk is crucial. The substance and style of teacher talk can have an influence on student academic language development. The content and form of teacher talk are known to have direct and indirect effects on students' communication skills. Bailie (2015) argued that communication, engagement, presence, timeliness, responsiveness, and modeling are positively related to online student satisfaction. These practices also apply to onsite student satisfaction. In fact, teachers' actions, behaviors, demeanors, and temperaments play a significant role in making students active or passive participants.

Teaching in the United States as an Immigrant

A sizeable number of immigrant teachers contribute qualified experiences, talents, and expertise to the American education system. According to a 2019 report by the Institute for Immigration Research, 11% of K–12 teachers in the United States are foreign-born (Furuya et al., 2019). Yet, immigrants make up only approximately 13% of the U.S. population. Spread throughout the country, they have different statuses: Some immigrant teachers are naturalized American citizens, some are permanent residents, and some have temporary work visas. Overall, their contribution is paramount and cannot be underestimated. The cultural, pedagogical, organizational, educational, linguistic, and technological diversity they bring to bear on the task of educating American students and preparing the future U.S. workforce is enriching, uplifting, and invaluable. They bring a mix of skills and knowledge that immensely benefits K–12 education and beyond. Their lasting contributions have been considerably demonstrated. Their overrepresentation in teaching in U.S. higher education institutions has been widely reported and documented (Furuya et al., 2019; Startz, 2017).

Teaching in the United States is a unique experience. Any immigrant considering teaching in an American public or private school needs to learn about the American educational system, the American multifaceted culture, and American core values. Before stepping into a classroom, it is important to have enhanced knowledge of what teaching entails and what to expect from American students. No matter how long you have lived in this country, no matter how rich your educational background is, no matter how experienced you are as a teacher, and no matter what your country of origin is, you still need to make important pedagogical and cultural adjustments. I remember my American stepdaughter advising me against accepting a teaching position in an American public school. She feared that I would not be able to handle American students.

The social status of teachers varies from one country to another. Although teachers enjoy a relative degree of respectability in the United States, it is worth noting that teaching as such is not regarded as a top-tier job. According to the 2018 Global Teacher

Status Index by the Varkey Foundation, which surveyed 35 countries, teaching is ranked the highest in status in China, Malaysia, Taiwan, Russia, Indonesia, South Korea, Turkey, and India, respectively. It is ranked 16th in the United States.

Recommended Resources

To be fully versed in K–12 education, it is important to study the essence and history of American education and key educational thinkers who have shaped the American education system. Sadker and Sadker (2000) provided the names of American education Hall of Fame contributors. Table 6 summarizes their contributions.

Table 6. Education Hall of Fame

Thinker	Contribution
Jean Jacques Rousseau	Stages of development
Comenius	Development stages of learning
Johann Heinrich Pestalozzi	Special needs of the disadvantaged
Friedrich Froebel	Kindergarten as an integral part of a child's education
Johann Herbart	Structured methodology of instruction
Emma Hart Willard	Opening doors of higher education to women
Horace Mann	Establishing free public schools
Prudence Crandall	Bringing education to African-American girls
Maria Montessori	Environment where young children could learn
John Dewey	Incorporating democratic practices in the educational process
Jean Piaget	Theory of cognitive development

Thinker	Contribution
Burrhus Frederick Skinner	Establishing a technology for teaching
Mary McLeod Bethune	Moving people from intellectual slavery to education
Paulo Freire	Efforts to mobilize education in the cause of social justice
Kenneth Clark	Effects of racism on all American children
Sylvia Ashton-Warner	Placing children at the center of the curriculum
Jerome Brunner	American school of cognitive psychology

Note. From *Teachers, Schools, and Society* (5th ed., pp. 301–312), by M. P. Sadker and D. M. Sadker, 2000, McGraw-Hill Companies, Inc. Copyright 2000 by McGraw-Hill Companies, Inc.

Clearly, there is a plethora of resources for teachers regarding literacy development, student engagement, rigor, questioning techniques (such as Bloom's taxonomy, Robert Marzano's Questioning Strategies), classroom management (such as restorative practices, EXCEL Model, and Yale Center RULER), authentic assessment, relationship building, critical thinking, literacy development, and effective teaching. Additionally, teachers can use a wide range of electronic resources to have a broader impact, including searchable databases, collaboration tools, synchronous and asynchronous communication tools, digital maps, virtual tour tools, learning management systems, student information systems, and so forth. The resources in Table 7 can make one's teaching experience in the United States easier.

Table 7. Useful Resources for Teachers

Resource	Examples
Searchable databases	Gale Virtual Reference Library, Infotopia, SIRS Knowledge Source, EBSCOhost, Google Scholar
Student information systems	PowerSchool SIS, Gradelink, Infinite Campus, Administrator's Plus, Skyward Student Management Suite
Collaboration tools	Zoom, Microsoft Teams, Miro, MindMeister, Loom
Interactive digital maps	Google Earth, Maptive, Mapbox
Video conferencing tools	Skype for Classroom, Telepresence
Learning management systems	Blackboard, Canvas, Edmodo, Schoology, Google Classroom, Diigo
Virtual field trips	360 Cities, The Zoo, Nature Lab
Video blogs	YouTube, TikTok, Instagram, Udemy
Weblogs	Evernote, Canva
Virtual team collaboration	Google Drive, Nectar, PeerSpace, Padlet, Jamboard
Multimedia presentation tools	PowerPoint, NearPod, PearDeck, Slideshare, Powtoon, Prezi
Translation tools/ESL tools	Duolingo, Babbl, Google Translate, Rosetta Stone
Interactive boards	Voicethread, Padlet, Jamboard
Discussion forums	Classroom Salon, Socrative
Instructional videos	Discovery Education, Crash Course Videos
Tutoring session tools	Blackboard Collaborate
Information sharing tools	Dropbox, Google Drive, OneDrive
Digital literacy	P21.org, EasyBib, Diigo
Screencasting tools	Screencastify, OBS Studio, Screencast-O-Matic
Interactive presentation tools	PearDeck, NearPod
Coding tools	CodeCombat, CodePen, Code Academy, Udemy, W3Schools, Code Hero, Code.org, CodeHS
Collaborative writing	Writeboard, Write with, Book Creator, Mixbook

Resource	Examples
Social networking tools	Yammer, LinkedIn, Google Meet, Twitter, Threads
Video editing	iMovie, Adobe Premiere, Sumovideo, ScreenPal
Concept maps/ brainstorming tools	Bubbl.us, Mindomo, Visme, Canva
Grant resources	Grants.gov, National Science Foundations
Scholarship resources	Scholarships.com, Fastweb, CollegeBoard, ScholarshipOwl, CareerOneStop

Miscommunication in the Classroom

It would be safe to assume that every immigrant teacher teaching in an American public or private K–12 school in the United States has faced a set of communication challenges. Theoretically, the seeds for these challenges emanate from the makeup of the classroom and teacher unpreparedness. Most induction programs or new teacher orientation programs do not emphasize this aspect. Yet, communication is paramount to the success of the teaching–learning process. It is misleading to assume, as many educational leaders do that foreign-born teachers always fully grasp the intricacies and complexities of cross-cultural communication in the classroom. However fluent in English an immigrant teacher is, he or she still has a professional obligation to be grounded in various strands of cross-cultural and linguistic realities in the classroom.

Understandably, immigrant teachers are not the only group affected by this problem. With the flux of migration of teachers in the United States from one geographic region to another, cross-cultural communication problems are bound to happen. Teachers from the North are moving to the South, from the East are moving to the West, and vice versa. Unless cross-cultural differences are handled with patience and realism, they can result in miscommunication and confrontation.

The notion of confrontation or argument is inherently ubiquitous in the fabric of a heterogeneous classroom. A diversified K–12 classroom can be an ideal ground for culture confrontation, race confrontation, prejudice confrontation, social status confrontation, social affiliation confrontation, political beliefs confrontation, gender confrontation, sexual orientation confrontation, and religion confrontation. The classroom offers unique opportunities for students and teachers to check, test, and confront their own philosophical or stereotypical perceptions. Even when educators and learners engage in the educational endeavor in a non-adversarial frame of mind, the potential for confrontation still exists in the classroom. Unless there is adequate psychological and pedagogical preparation, such an environment can easily turn into unmanageable chaos, which can ultimately and adversely hamper the learning process.

Arguably, communication rituals vary from one country to another, from one culture to another, and from one social group to another. Tannen (1986) argued that conversational styles can affect the content and nature of a dialogue. By and large, this is similarly true in an educational setting. In many American public high schools where diversity of faculty and student body is the norm, differences in the content and style of communication may naturally result in miscommunication or misunderstanding.

Metalanguage Incidents

Incident 1:

As I was at my duty post one morning, I witnessed two students having an unusual handshake on the school campus. I found the handshake interesting and funny. I was fascinated by the complexity and dexterity of the handplay. I asked the students to do it again. I wanted a school counselor who was standing next to me at her duty post to see and admire it as I did. "Let me see that handshake again," I said with a smile.

"No. You think I am a gangbanger. I am not in a gang. You are trying to get us in trouble," one student said.

The idea of gang membership never crossed my mind. I was simply and genuinely interested in the uniqueness of the handshake. I tried to explain to the two students that I liked their unique handshake. But the students did not buy my explanation; they walked away, visibly upset at me. I was left baffled. "What just happened?" I wondered and laughed. The school counselor and I spent a few minutes discussing that particular instance of miscommunication and others in schools.

Incident 2:

A young man insistently asked me to help him with his assignment while I was helping another student. Instinctively and forgetting the cultural context, I used a hand gesture to ask him to wait, or so I thought.

The student took it to mean, "Talk to the hand. I am not talking to you." He took offense at the gesture and was furious. "You are going to shush me like that? This man does not know who he is messing with," he said.

I tried to explain to him that I wanted him to wait. The hand gesture means "wait" in my native country.

He was too upset to listen. "How long have you lived in this country? You should know by now what that gesture means. You are not going to disrespect me like that." It took a few minutes for the student to calm down.

Later, before the end of class, I had an opportunity to explain to him the rationale behind the use of the hand gesture. I told him that, sometimes, I just instinctively resort to some natural reflexes, such as using certain hand gestures or using my native language.

Incident 3:

Traditionally, the class often analyzed, critiqued, and/or reviewed games they played on iPads, mobile phones, 3DX, game consoles, desktops, or laptops. One day, my students were playing different types of board and electronic games in a Game Art and Design class. As they were playing in small groups, a Hispanic student in one of the groups exclaimed, "Stupid nigger!" He uttered these two words every time he failed to remove a piece or had limited options in a Jumbo Towers game. He played with two students: another Hispanic student and an African-American student. The class had a mixture of African-American students (8), Hispanic students (5), and Asian students (1).

Some of the African-American students signaled their disapproval by yelling, "What?"

A couple of them came to his defense: "He is one of us; it is okay."

The teacher seized the opportunity to discuss cultural sensitivity. The offender argued that he always used that phrase, even in front of his African-American friends, and none of them seemed to be bothered by it.

Some of my African-American students discouraged the use of such a phrase, which they found to be offensive. I asked the Hispanic student about the meaning he attached to the phrase "stupid nigger." He stated it simply meant a stupid mistake.

Whether this was a simple case of gullibility or a manifestation of an internalized prejudice is hard to decrypt. Interestingly, the student understood the teacher's brief lecture about the meaning and history of the word "nigger" and promised not to use it any longer. Paradoxically, some African-American students in the class loved to use the N-word as a sign of endearment among friends and, sometimes, as an insult. They argued there was a phonetic difference that was only perceptible to insiders (Black people). They warned outsiders (other races) to refrain from using the N-word. If outsiders used the word, it would be at their own peril, and they might end up with stitches. I always found that rationale strange!

This scene offered a perfect opportunity for the teacher to leverage the power of a positive confrontation. Dodge (2019) recommended that students should learn to engage in difficult conversations. An open dialogue was initiated. Students argued for and against the offensive occurrence. The perpetrator learned at the end that the phrase was inappropriate. He promised not to use it any longer and admitted he was so used to it that he never knew it was hurtful. Positive confrontation had the merit of resolving the miscommunication.

Incident 4:

I had my first taste of miscommunication with an American woman in 1995 in Kinshasa, the capital city of the Democratic Republic of the Congo. An American friend returned from a trip to Switzerland, where she had gone to attend a conference. I had not seen her for quite some time. We met a few days after her European trip. I complimented her (or so I thought) in front of a group of onlookers (some of them American) on her look: "You look great! You gained some weight!"

> Her unenthusiastic "thank you" did not mean much to me until a Congolese who worked for the American embassy told me after the woman walked away, "You should never say something like that to an American woman. Did you see how she reacted?"
>
> Back then, I had very little experience with the American popular culture. I spoke English but was unaware of that aspect of the American culture. In my home country, it was quite customary for people to congratulate one another on weight gain. They still do, to some extent. This is viewed as a form of compliment.

Since the aforementioned incident, I have witnessed several other instances of miscommunication between Americans and foreigners. Nonverbal cues may also lead to miscommunication as they vary from one country to another. Finger crossing, for example, which means "bad luck" in my native country, is regarded as a sign of "good luck" in the United States. Hand clapping as an apology was hailed as an act of defiance in Orlando, Florida, by a White man who expected me to hold the door for him when I first moved to the United States. Back then, I was not familiar with the American door-holding traditional courtesy. He was offended that I walked away without holding the door for him, and he expressed his disapproval of my "discourtesy."

These unpleasant experiences opened my eyes to the communication gap that a lack of cultural context can engender. My suggestion is that foreign language learning should not be dissociated with cultural contextualization. Many EFL (English as a Foreign Language) or ESL books focus more on the understanding and manipulation of the target language than on the link between language and culture. Moreover, there is scant exposure of non-native EFL or ESL teachers to standard native English. Fortunately, several electronic tools now enable EFL/ESL learners to access a variety of multimedia resources in the target language.

Action Research by Teachers

The strategic value of action research by educational practitioners to construct practical solutions to educational problems cannot be overstated (Mertler, 2021). As insiders, teachers are the prime actors of the pedagogical actions they undertake and the prime eyewitnesses of the sociocognitive responses that follow in the classroom. No other individuals are closer to classroom realities than teachers. Unfortunately, rarely have I seen K–12 teachers engage in active, useful action research in the United States. Despite their daily interactions with students and the vast stock of student data that teachers have access to through a wide range of student information systems and other databases, there is a dearth of teacher-driven research. Yet, available data can be mined to better understand enabling and inhibiting factors to teaching effectiveness. Definitionally, *action research* is a systematic, intentional investigation of one's professional action conducted by educational practitioners to enrich teaching and learning practices (Dana & Yendol-Hoppey, 2019; Woolfolk, 2004). As a means of enhancing teaching effectiveness, action research can be a critical driver of innovations in the classroom in that it helps pinpoint unique strengths and weaknesses of the teaching and learning processes. However, teachers are not known for being active action researchers. Yet, teaching can and, indeed, does benefit from action research.

Two reasons appear to be most plausible. One reason is lack of time. Research can be expensive and time-consuming (Woolfolk, 2004). Teaching is a demanding profession, and teachers are often swamped with large amounts of work: planning lessons, attending PD activities, grading assignments, unpacking standards, learning new skills, exploring new resources, reaching out to parents, examining students' needs, building relationships with students, delivering instruction, reflecting on instruction effectiveness, and managing student behaviors. This is just a synopsis of the work teachers do. They are left with little or no time to engage in complex action research. It is worth noting that action research has four stages: planning, acting, developing, and reflecting (Mertler, 2021). Another reason is the lack of adequate preparation. Based on experience, it looks as though teachers are not sufficiently trained to engage in systematic investigations involving data collection, data analysis, and reporting of results. It has been opined that teacher education programs tend to prepare teachers to be consumers rather than producers of applied classroom-based research.

Furthermore, even though most educational leaders recognize the value of action research that qualified scholars produce, several school districts do not focus on teacher-generated action research. In some cases, scholars who produce research aimed at improving teaching quality have little or no classroom teaching experience. Teachers are often handed a synopsis of research findings for informational purposes or to translate into action in the classroom. In fact, a considerable amount of classroom-based research is carried out by non-classroom educational scholars, far removed from daily classroom occurrences. Moreover, a great deal of action research that is published, including doctoral action research, is not available to teachers.

Although many CTE teachers are not known to be versed in action research, their insights and firsthand perspectives may help unearth a wealth of information that can shed further light on classroom realities and ultimately lead to the improvement of the teaching–learning process. Undertaking small-scale research, even while using convenience samples, can help teachers improve different aspects of their teaching. Research has shown that teachers are more effective when they reflect on their teaching practices. In addition to instructional strategies, preservice training, and PD sessions should emphasize the mastery of research methods such as observations, case studies, diaries, questionnaires, interviews, and document analysis. Teachers should be encouraged to use convenience samples for their research, with particular emphasis on reliability, validity, and consistency. Despite their pitfalls, convenience samples have their merits.

There is a plethora of topics that teachers can investigate. Teachers should be encouraged to reflect on their teaching practices. They can examine how their own teaching styles affect their students' academic achievement, how microaggressions affect student attendance, how different protocols enhance student engagement, how reading strengthens reading skills, how effective recommended resources and instructional strategies are, and how students learn best. They may also be interested in causal factors that contribute to *social loafing*, defined as the tendency for some students to put in less effort than their full potential in group work (Latané et al., 1979). In any case, teachers who engage in action research are likely to be reflective thinkers who assess and reassess their teaching practices with an improvement goal in mind. Action research should be shared, critiqued, peer-reviewed (if necessary), and even replicated. By default, as teaching is a collaborative endeavor, action research should not be done in isolation or in a vacuum. Instead, it should be incentivized (financially), encouraged, and promoted.

It is my view that a considerable part of teacher preparation programs should focus on initiating teachers-in-action research. Teachers have access to a large amount of data encompassing student performance, school improvement plans, key performance indicators, truancy, and learning needs. It is only fitting that they conduct research from time to time to gauge the effectiveness of their performance. If they do not conduct research, they can at least point researchers to certain aspects of research that can benefit them or participate in research endeavors in some capacity.

Table 8 is a sample of a basic assessment data analysis that a teacher can conduct. I conducted this brief analysis several years ago using actual data from students' test scores to assess the link between student attendance and test scores for one unit. IDs have been removed to preserve students' confidentiality. Proficiency level 1 marks failure. Proficiency level 2 shows success.

Table 8. Breakdown of Students' Grades and Absences

Student Gender	Grade Level	Student ID	Quarter 1		Proficiency Level
			Absences	Grade	
M	12	0000000	4	98	2
M	10	0000000	3	96	2
M	9	0000000	5	50	1
F	9	0000000	4	54	1
M	10	0000000	5	96	2
M	11	0000000	4	86	2
M	9	0000000	0	86	2
F	11	0000000	3	92	2
M	10	0000000	3	98	2
M	9	0000000	1	90	2
M	11	0000000	6	96	2
F	9	0000000	5	100	2
M	12	0000000	1	100	2
M	10	0000000	3	96	2
M	10	0000000	2	100	2
F	9	0000000	5	90	2
M	11	0000000	3	98	2
F	9	0000000	5	92	2
F	11	0000000	0	100	2

Using Excel or Microsoft Word, teachers can review and cross-examine assessment data and draw conclusions. Data from this simple contingency table can be examined in several ways: gender vs. proficiency levels, attendance vs. proficiency levels, attendance vs. grade levels, grades vs. grade levels, and so forth. The key hypothesis of the study was that class attendance is positively correlated with a student's academic achievement. A survey of influence effectiveness was used to gauge a teacher's influence on students with attendance problems. It was assumed the teacher plays a critical role in influencing a student's perspective on class attendance. The influence and importance of several other critical factors that contribute to a student's success, including parental involvement, student's personal commitment, school characteristics, and student characteristics, were also examined. It was argued that class attendance has a direct effect on student academic performance. By examining this important issue, such a small-scale study can help heighten understanding of the various dimensions of attendance, factors influencing class attendance, challenges that can impede learning, and the relationship between attendance and academic achievement.

Professional Development Imperative

Teaching, in essence, is a complex process in which teachers have the responsibility to create conditions conducive to learning. This requires them to be sufficiently and continuously trained to face a variety of challenges, notably the ever-expanding student demographics, ever-changing instructional materials and technologies, diversity of students' abilities, broad array of students' needs, experiences, and cultural values, and students' learning styles. No matter how prepared the teacher is when entering the profession, he or she still has a duty to upgrade his or her skills. Teachers who fail to upgrade their skills become less competitive and less productive and consequently can be marginalized. They must constantly adapt to change—new curricular options, new leadership vision, new insights, new pedagogical standards, new instructional strategies, new research findings, and new technologies. The quality of PD activities must be tied to specific needs for professional growth. Teachers sometimes wonder, "Is it worth my time?" They can be working on other activities during that time. Teachers should not be overloaded or overburdened with PD activities that are irrelevant to their jobs. Relevant PD activities must be tailored to enhance the quality of instruction because effective instruction is known to be a predictor of student engagement and achievement (Scott et al., 2014). Essentially, there must be an assessment of learning needs or professional growth needs prior to deciding the types of PD activities teachers should participate in. Every teacher can contribute to the selection of PD activities and PD facilitators. No teacher is so knowledgeable or experienced that he or she has nothing new to learn. Likewise, no teacher is such an empty vessel that he or she has nothing to share.

Conclusion

In conclusion, it is imperative that foreign-born teachers adjust to the culture and teaching practices in the United States. These cultural and pedagogical adjustments may concern the way they interact, communicate, socialize, engage with, and respond to American students. I have seen teachers teach and interact with American students the way they would in their native countries. Some teachers tend to contextualize course content by drawing examples from their native countries, which may put American students at a loss.

It should be noted that American students should not be lumped into one monolithic behavioral or personality category. Individually, students are different. However, it has been my experience that a good number of American students will not hesitate to voice their opinions about how they feel about a teacher or a class or about virtually anything. A foreign-born teacher must be prepared to deal with this type of directness and blunt honesty, which at times might be raw, casual, and uncomfortable. Cultural knowledge will serve foreign-born teachers well. They should demonstrate the ability to handle discipline problems and to cope with diverse learners with different personalities and abilities.

Of course, there are several differences between the way you approach teaching in your native country and the way you should approach teaching in the United States. You are dealing with different students in a completely different educational environment. Regardless of your teaching experience and qualifications, there is a learning curve you must go through. It is important that you explore common teaching practices, common learning activities and styles, effective classroom management techniques, and ancillary teaching resources. What may have worked elsewhere will not necessarily work here. Be open to learning and to welcome constructive feedback. Your effectiveness as a teacher is judged on a host of qualities and characteristics, which include professional knowledge, instructional planning, instructional delivery, assessment, learning environment, and professionalism (Stronge, 2018).

Finally, it is crucial to acknowledge the work of immigrant teachers in due course. I have witnessed immigrant teachers leaving at the end of their contracts without receiving a simple verbal or written thank-you from school administrators. Some have retired in complete silence. This lack of gratitude is inhumane and unwelcoming.

SECTION 3

Bolstering Teachers' Professional Identity: A Look at Teacher Compensation Plans

Introduction

The chapters in this section, which focus on the examination of teacher payment plans, address critical issues related to teachers' underpayment and the paradox of linking teacher pay to teacher performance, given the multifaceted nature of teacher performance. They illustrate what teachers make and plead for teachers' professional identity rehabilitation through decent incentive plans. They also highlight some negative consequences of teachers' extra employment. Taken together, the two chapters exemplify the tremendous pressures teachers face to perform optimally.

Chapter 7, "A Critical Appraisal of Teacher Renumeration," examines teacher compensation plans considering existing data. Specifically, it addresses the need for rehabilitating the teaching profession, reasons why society seems to have turned its back on teachers, what teachers make, challenges with teacher retention due to teacher underpayment, reasons why teachers quit their jobs, students' views of teacher pay, teacher workload versus pay disparity, consequences of extra employment, and teacher pay versus stress levels. Throughout the chapter, these issues are explored from insiders' perspectives as well as from extant literature.

Chapter 8, "The Paradox of Teacher Performance Operationalization," tackles the daunting debate about linking teacher pay to teacher performance. It revisits the notion of teacher effectiveness and explores the complex question of pay-for-performance plan versus teacher performance. The chapter ends with practical recommendations for bolstering teachers' professional identity, and, thereby, retaining effective teachers.

Chapter 7

A Critical Appraisal of Teacher Remuneration

Teacher Compensation: Rehabilitating the Teaching Profession

Let me begin with an anecdotal tale of an incident involving a teacher who attempted to marry his beloved fiancée in a country in central Africa. The teacher and his fiancée were deeply in love, the story goes. The fiancée's family was wealthy and greatly charmed by the teacher's physique and intellect. One day, the fiancée's mother wondered about her daughter's fiancé's job: "My daughter, I have never asked you about my future son-in-law's job. What does he do for a living?" she asked. Her daughter replied joyfully, "I apologize for not telling you earlier. He is a teacher." Shocked, the mother sternly remarked, "So he does not have a real job. How can he marry you, then?" she asked. "No, Mom, he does have a job. I just told you that he is a teacher," the daughter replied. Exasperated, the mother concluded that she would not allow her daughter to marry a poor teacher.

This view paints a rather alarming picture of teaching. To this wealthy woman, teaching is not a full-fledged profession; it is a non-job. In fact, she is not the only person to hold this opinion. A large portion of the population in my native country no longer considers teaching the noble profession it used to be in the 1950s, 1960s, and 1970s. Rare are parents who are comfortable having a teacher as a son-in-law.

Here is a scene I found fascinating. Inside a Walmart store in Huntersville, North Carolina, I saw a parent arguing with her 7- or 8-year-old son over a gift for an unnamed teacher during Teacher Appreciation Week.

> Boy: "I want to buy my teacher a present for teacher appreciation. Can I have some money, please?"
>
> The mother replied angrily, "No, why should I buy your teacher something? What has she bought for me?"
>
> The boy went on to say, "I already told her I would bring her a present tomorrow."
>
> The mother inflexibly replied, "Tell her you don't have money."

Overhearing the conversation as a teacher, I almost invited myself into the conversation but decided not to due to the parent's harsh tone of voice. I felt like telling her that a thank-you letter could go a long way to show appreciation to a teacher. Teachers do not always expect presents but do take special pride in reading thank-you letters from students, parents, and school leaders. This parent might never realize the teacher's intangible deeds that earned her the boy's trust. There have been cases of teachers retiring or leaving, heartbroken, without anyone thanking them for their service.

Has Society Turned Its Back on Teachers?

One of the greatest mysteries of modern times is how teaching has lost its nobility. In many parts of the world, teachers are not regarded as decent-salaried employees who can provide for their families. This portrayal is in stark contrast with Nobel Prize winner John Steinbeck's (1952) depiction of an ideal teacher in his novel *East of Eden*:

> In the country, the repository of art and science was the school, and the schoolteacher shielded and carried the torch of learning and of beauty. The schoolhouse was the meeting place for music, for debate... And the teacher was not only an intellectual paragon and a social leader but also the matrimonial catch of the countryside. A family could indeed walk proudly if a son married the schoolteacher. Her children were presumed to have intellectual advantages,, both inherited and conditioned. (p. 141)

In Steinbeck's Great American West, a teacher is a paragon of intellectual virtues. Thus, marrying a teacher would be a sign of pride rather than a curse. Unfortunately, this image of nobility has been tarnished over the years due to inadequate teacher compensation and insufficient funding of public education. Today, the term *teacher* conjures up images of poverty, demoralization, stress, marginalization, shame, and mockery. The 2014 Gallup report *State of America's Schools* described the teaching profession as being repeatedly "vilified" (Rath, 2014, p. 23) in the national debate. The teaching workforce is seen as a class of dedicated, skilled professionals who are vastly under-compensated and who fulfill their professional responsibilities under stringent conditions. Modest teacher pay, along with inadequate funding of education, may partly account for the current state of the U.S. education system. Gratz (2009) used such words as "*crisis, scandal, deplorable, wretched,* and *disgraceful*" (p. 113) to describe the U.S. education system.

Some education policymakers tend to trivialize the teaching profession and advocate for a status quo regarding teacher pay. I once watched a televised debate about education reform in North Carolina in which a lawmaker stated disparagingly, "No one enters teaching expecting to be rich. Teachers know that they are called to serve, not to be rich." He was opposed to a proposed teacher pay raise plan.

When I was teaching in a high school in the Democratic Republic of the Congo, teachers often complained about their salaries. Salaries were so insignificant that it was hard for a primary or secondary school teacher to make ends meet in the 1980s and 1990s. Teachers had to piece together part-time jobs in addition to their main job to manage their financial responsibilities. To make ends meet, some taught at two or three schools. I personally had to teach concurrently in two secondary schools in addition to tutoring adults and youngsters in their homes. Never had I imagined that American teachers had similar concerns, though on a different scale. I thought teacher remuneration was not a concern in the United States. True, teachers' salaries are quite significant in the United States compared to teachers' salaries in my native country. However, the cost of living, market value, and inflation adjustment seem to nullify the disparity.

On the surface, there is a sense of normalcy about teachers' living conditions in the United States. When I first started teaching in a public school in the United States, teachers did not exhibit an image of a poor class of professionals who begged for pity. The first time I visited an American high school, I was mesmerized by the quantity and quality of vehicles in the school parking lot and the state of the buildings. Teachers drove decent vehicles and dressed professionally. Even some students commuted to school in nice cars (though most students rode in school buses). I had the opportunity to visit some colleagues in their homes and was generally impressed. In my native country, I do not recall having seen a high school teacher in the late 1980s and early 1990s who owned a vehicle. Very few older teachers owned houses. It was extremely hard for a teacher to save, let alone buy a house or a vehicle. Yet, in the 1960s and 1970s, when 1 Congolese franc was worth 2 U.S. dollars, teachers were highly regarded. They lived decently and were greatly respected. They were models of our society because there were very few intellectuals with an educational background. Although their salaries were not colossal, they had enough to live on.

Underpaying teachers is a disservice to students who do not get the best out of their teachers. Demoralized and dissatisfied, a good number of teachers leave the profession they dearly love each year in the United States. All things considered, it looks as though this super-powerful country has turned its back on teachers. It is important that teachers reclaim the moral rewards of their noble profession (Santoro, 2011).

What Teachers Make

As a high school teacher in the United States, I was quickly dismayed by the reality of teacher underpayment. In fact, teachers were paid less than professionals with similar qualifications (Odden & Kelley, 2002). García and Weiss (2019) reported that teachers earn 60% of what a professional with comparable education does. According to the National Center for Education Statistics, the national average annual salary of teachers in public elementary and secondary schools in 2022–2023 was **$57,805, even though** some school districts pay teachers an annual salary that can exceed $80,000 (Odden

& Kelley, 2002). The median annual wage for high school teachers was $62,360 in May 2022, according to the Bureau of Labor Statistics (2023). The National Education Association (NEA, 2023), the largest teachers union in the country, noted that the national average teacher pay for the 2022–2023 school year was $68,469. Seemingly, not much has changed since 1999, when the national average teacher pay was $40,574 (Odden & Kelley, 2002). If enacted into law, the American Teacher Act, which guarantees a minimum annual salary of $60,000 for all teachers nationwide, might help change perceptions and have a positive impact on teacher retention. This would be a positive step forward. However, it may not be as significant with growing inflation.

Challenges With Teacher Retention

There is no denying that teachers' satisfaction is linked in part to teacher pay. With respect to teachers' job satisfaction, evidence has shown an abrupt drop and an undercurrent of despair since 2009 (Koedel et al., 2017; Santoro, 2011). This may help explain the high rates of teacher attrition. Job satisfaction is known to be a key pillar of teacher retention. Odden and Kelley (2002) argued that high teacher pay is key to the recruitment and retention of quality teachers. The more satisfied teachers are, the more likely they are to remain in their jobs. This may explain the acute shortage of qualified teachers, especially in the STEM fields. Many CTE courses, for example, are taught by teachers without a technical background. Highly qualified professionals with the right credentials are more likely to choose professions that remunerate them better than teaching would. To face this challenge, some school districts hire teachers without proper qualifications and train them through mentoring/coaching, pedagogical preparation, induction, and continuous PD. Moreover, they recruit teachers with required credentials from other countries, such as South Africa, the Philippines, Jamaica, and Japan.

Teacher retention and teacher attrition continue to be major challenges for many school districts in the United States, especially in urban schools. Nearly 15% of the teaching workforce is moving or leaving every year. American teachers are leaving the profession before retirement age at higher rates compared to other countries, such as Finland and Singapore. Over the past decade, roughly 8% of American teachers left the workforce (Sutcher et al., 2019). Why are there such shortages? Sutcher et al. (2016) noted four main factors drive that teacher shortages: a decline in teacher preparation enrollments, district efforts to return to prerecessionpupil–teacher ratios, increasing student enrollment, and high teacher attrition. Billingsley (1993) postulated that there are three broad contributing factors to high teacher turnover: personal factors, external factors, and employment factors. Personal factors include gender, race, age group, marital status, education level, teacher qualifications, certification or endorsement, academic ability, and teacher preparation. External factors include family support and parental/community support. Employment factors consist of administrative support, colleague or central office support, stress, role conflict, ambiguity, commitment, job satisfaction, induction and mentoring programs, and involvement.

Why Teachers Leave Their Jobs

Over the years, I have had opportunities to inquire about teacher attrition from teachers exiting CMS. Many teachers have suggested that it all boils down to job dissatisfaction due to modest teacher pay, students' misbehaviors, unfair treatment, lack of parental support, lack of professional objectivity, and lack of instructional support. With regard to the shortage of qualified teachers, 85% of school districts in the United States reported an immediate demand for qualified and experienced teachers in the areas of STEM. Sutcher et al. (2016) noted that four main factors drive teacher shortages: a decline in teacher preparation enrollments, district efforts to return to prerecession student–teacher ratios, increasing student enrollment, and high teacher attrition. Papay et al. (2017) surveyed 16 school districts in seven states and found that 55% of novice teachers in urban schools leave their district, and 70% leave their school within 5 years. Breaux and Wong (2003) probed reasons why teachers leave and summarized seven causal factors from the literature: (a) lack of support, (b) disenchantment with teaching assignments, (c) difficulty balancing personal and professional demands, (d) excessive paperwork, (e) inadequate classroom management, (f) inadequate discipline, and (g) high stress. Paradoxically, research suggests that the most academically skilled teachers exit the profession in larger proportions than less academically gifted teachers (Breaux & Wong, 2003). This finding is corroborated by a study conducted by Hare and Heap (2001) from the North Central Regional Education Laboratory that found the majority of the teachers (75–100%) who exited the profession were rated as *effective* or *very effective*.

While there have been significant efforts in some states to improve teachers' pay, a few states have been cutting teachers' pay. Unbecomingly, some states have allowed teachers' salaries to stagnate for over a decade despite rising inflation. The recent wave of protests in North Carolina, Arizona, West Virginia, Kentucky, Colorado, and Oklahoma by teachers demanding pay raises and more funding for education only articulate the severity of the situation. The perception of teaching with its cohort of problems does not incentivize some young, well-educated professionals to join the teaching workforce.

In a 2001 study conducted by University of Pennsylvania researcher Richard Ingersoll using the USDE's Teacher Follow-Up

Survey, it was reported that, for teachers who left high-poverty schools because of job dissatisfaction, low salary was a primary reason for leaving. Chait and Miller (2009) noted teachers cited compensation (56%) more frequently than any other factor as the primary reason for leaving rural high-poverty schools. Conversely, poor administrative support (50.1%) and lack of faculty influence (42.5%) were cited as the main factors for teachers leaving urban high-poverty schools.

Thus, teacher retention in high-poverty schools is relatively low. Compression of teacher wages in the United States is another important reason for the decline in teacher quality, with higher-ability teachers exiting the teacher labor market (Hoxby & Leigh, 2004). Ultimately, teacher pay and work conditions are two reasons why teachers leave the profession.

Students' Views of Teacher Pay

Throughout my teaching career, I have had opportunities to discuss with students their views regarding teaching. Some of the students shared some disturbing thoughts about teacher pay.

> "I heard that a garbage collector makes more money than a teacher. Is it true?"
>
> "They don't pay teachers enough, so why are you a teacher?"
>
> "You guys are highly educated. Why are you selling yourself so short?"
>
> "I can never become a teacher. I do not have the patience to deal with kids. And I do not want to die poor."
>
> "You are a smart Black man. You can have a much better job if you want to. We all know that teachers are treated like garbage

in this country! Why are you wasting your time dealing with these bad kids?"

"A garbage collector makes more than a teacher."

"Basically, I can pay you. My job pays better than yours. I am still a student, but I drive a better car than you."

These statements and questions seem to be innocent and naïve by nature. Yet, they specifically encapsulate students' apprehension toward the teaching profession. Moreover, they reveal genuine concerns about teachers' well-being. If students perceive their teachers as poor professionals who can barely survive on their income, then this perception can ultimately affect their college or employment choices. The caricature-like image of teaching helps explain why colleges are having trouble attracting students into their educational programs and why fewer Americans are enrolling in teaching career programs.

Workload vs. Pay Disparity

The dichotomy between the amount of work teachers are required to shoulder, and teacher compensation seems paradoxical. It is no secret that teachers are massively overburdened with work. However, they are not adequately compensated for all the work they are required to do. Based on their research on effective instruction, Rosenshine and Stevens (1986, 1995) summarized six main teaching functions: (a) review and check the previous day's work, (b) present new material, (c) provide guided practice, (d) give feedback and correctives based on student answers, (e) provide independent practice, and (f) review weekly and monthly to consolidate learning.

In reality, teachers are expected to complete many more duties, namely, working on lesson plans, grading student assignments, evaluating and documenting student progress, providing personalized feedback, motivating students, mentoring/coaching colleagues/students, attending mandatory PD activities and meetings, completing licensure requirements, preparing and distributing progress reports/report cards, taking students on field trips, preparing summative and formative assessments, facilitating workshops, creating conditions for active learning, participating in PLC meetings, counseling students, attending testing training sessions, tracking students' data, maintaining a clean learning environment, reviewing educational research, managing classes to optimize learning opportunities, collaborating with colleagues, exploring and accommodating students' needs, communicating with parents, conducting learning walkthroughs, attending educational events and activities, and delivering instruction.

Yet, they are often blamed for student academic failure or underachievement. Most people who fault teachers for student failure do not realize how complex and multifaceted teaching is. Teaching, which is regarded as the mother of all professions, is uniquely different from other professions. Being able to deal with classroom realities requires a special skill set—a mix of patience, flexibility, adaptability, open-mindedness, and devotion. It defies common sense that, despite this excessive workload, teachers still have to constantly pressure decision-makers into rethinking their compensation systems. A country that values its teachers would never allow them to work extra jobs just to meet their basic needs.

Consequences of Extra Employment

Job dissatisfaction correlates with teacher stress levels, which can erode teacher effectiveness. Evidently, poor teacher pay can amplify the erosion or fragility of teacher effectiveness by forcing teachers to find additional streams of income. I spoke with several teachers who reported having a second or third job because it was financially draining to live on one income. "I can't make it with my salary alone. I have a family to feed," one teacher said. Another teacher told me, "I can't afford to lose my second job. Without it, I can't survive." In fact, most teachers I know have part-time jobs in addition to teaching. They cannot meet their financial obligations with a single source of income. Teachers are 30 percent more likely to have a second job than the average full-time worker. To put it into perspective, this is the highest percentage reported in over a decade. Moreover, it is, to some extent, greater than it was at the height of the Great Recession. The subsequent demands of two or three jobs in terms of time and energy can adversely and significantly impact the teacher's effectiveness in doing the extra work required to provide first-rate instruction. A teacher whose second job ends at 10:00 or 11:00 in the evening is likely to encounter problems with lesson planning, resource gathering, attendance, energy, and staying awake in the classroom. This can lead to inefficiency, stress, and physical burnout.

Clearly, the consequences of juggling multiple jobs can be horrendous. Poor teacher pay has a profound impact on job satisfaction. If teachers cannot depend on their wages to meet their basic needs, then teaching can become a stressful profession. A huge body of research argues that there is a link between stress and teaching effectiveness. While low-stress levels can positively affect teacher effectiveness, high-stress levels may lead to ineffective teaching practices.

Undoubtedly, ineffective teaching practices affect student learning outcomes. As research has shown, there is a link not only between teacher stress and teacher effectiveness but also between teacher stress and student learning outcomes. Educational scholars and practitioners agree that high-stress levels can negatively affect teaching and learning. Herman et al. (2018) pointed out that high levels of teacher job-related stress result in poor student outcomes. By default, teaching is an exciting profession. However, it comes with an array of challenges. Coping with mixed-ability students, large class sizes, students' conduct, lack of parental involvement, and inadequate resources can altogether be a highly daunting task.

Another negative consequence, especially in CTE, is that qualified teachers in certain fields, such as computer programming, manufacturing, engineering, and graphic design, to name a few, prefer other jobs. This leaves schools with teachers who do not have the educational background and have to attend several workshops to gain the skills required to teach those classes.

The demands of teaching are draining. There are a few professions that pummel employees into continuing education training, certification training, PLC meetings, department meetings, general faculty meetings, PD training (literacy development, student engagement, classroom management), new courses, and testing training like teaching does. Whether for credit renewal, dissatisfaction with the administration, disrespect from students, licensure requirements, low salary, or lack of support, many teachers have been forced to quit the job they so dearly love. By improving some of these conditions, beginning with teacher pay, maybe the teaching profession will be able to attract more caring souls willing to impact young lives. Retaining high-performing teachers can be surprisingly simple or dauntingly complex, depending on how school leaders approach the issue. Recommended actions for teacher retention include offering competitive salaries, treating teachers with professional respect, decreasing the amount of paperwork, providing instructional support, and acknowledging teachers' professional contributions.

Teacher Pay vs. Stress Levels

The notion of job security for teachers should not be confined to basic physiological needs—food, water, and shelter. If teachers cannot fulfill other important human needs, such as health care, transportation, mortgage or rent, and childcare, it is hard for them to be fully committed to providing value-added instruction to students. Teachers should be able to rely on their earnings to fulfill their financial duties. They should not have to worry about how they are going to get to work, what they are going to eat, how they are going to pay their mortgage or rent, how they are going to take care of their families, and so forth. Let's not make teaching any more stressful than it already is by underpaying teachers and expecting them to overachieve. As human beings, they can only offer what they can within the bounds of their human capabilities.

Most jobs leave employees time to focus on other occupational or parental duties. Teaching consumes time beyond work hours. Devoted teachers spend a considerable amount of time planning learning activities. They have to scavenge or gather an assortment of resources they need to teach. They have to find the most effective instructional strategies that can produce positive results. They have to think about ways to best instill in students the drive to learn and furnish extrinsic motivation. Furthermore, they have to reflect on their teaching practices.

Arguably, a society that values education remunerates its teachers accordingly. It secures subsequent investments in the education sector. Given the strategic importance of education, it is only fitting that teachers be compensated decently. Teaching requires a time commitment, devotion, specialized expertise that takes years to achieve, instructional support, and psychological and pedagogical preparation. It is immensely paramount to society because it guides cognitive growth, sharpens intellect, and enhances personal development. In today's competitive world, underpaying teachers and overburdening them with excessive workload can be a recipe for underachievement for teachers as well as for students. The centrality of the teacher's role in student learning is demonstrably vital. Assuming that salary is one of the main reasons why fewer young people are not interested in joining the teaching workforce, it would seem reasonable to compensate teachers adequately. Thus, rethinking compensation policies is a step toward the rehabilitation of this noble profession.

Chapter 8

The Paradox of Teacher Performance Operationalization

Teacher Effectiveness Revisited

The debate over teacher effectiveness often centers on direct learning outcomes. Through the narrow prism of average improvement in expected student gains, specifically in terms of standardized test scores for a whole class or school (Goe et al., 2008; Woolfolk, 2004), the real meaning of teacher effectiveness is distorted. Teacher effectiveness cannot and should not be assessed solely in relation to measurable student outcomes (Blanton et al., 2006), as student test scores are never the only key performance indicator. It is a professional blunder to encapsulate teacher effectiveness in this one measure. There is evidence that a teacher can harness outstanding results with one group of learners based on some demographic characteristics (socioeconomic status, gender, age, religion, or race); however, the same teacher may be ineffective in a different context with a different set of learners.

Teacher effectiveness is multilayered. Day et al. (2008) proposed a model of teacher effectiveness with several contributing factors: (a) individual characteristics, (b) student characteristics, (c) school or department factors, (d) student attainment, and (e) policy reforms. Individual characteristics include self, self-efficacy, career, and locus of control. Student characteristics include motivation, ability, and external social influences. School or department factors are leadership, culture, classroom organization, and teaching. Student attainment involves student attitudes to learning and long-term achievements. Finally, policy reforms are about conditions of service, expectations, standards, beliefs, and values. Holistically, these characteristics should play a role in assessing teacher effectiveness.

There is growing recognition that there are multiple indicators of teacher effectiveness beyond one single measure (test scores). To best assess the essence of teacher performance, Goe et al. (2008) proposed a broader array of evaluation instruments encompassing classroom observations, principal evaluation, instructional artifacts, portfolios, teacher self-report measures, student surveys, and value-added model. This list leaves out other indirect measures, such as teacher's mastery of content knowledge, teacher's responses to theoretical teaching situations, teacher's instructional presentations, teacher–student interplay, students' long-term academic or psychological impact, and parent satisfaction surveys.

Anita Woolfolk (2004), professor of educational psychology at Ohio State University, identified three teacher characteristics that are determinants of effective teaching: knowledge, clarity and organization, and warmth and enthusiasm. Many studies have adopted an integrative and multilevel approach to teacher evaluation (Darling-Hammond, 2000; Day et al., 2008; Goe et al., 2008; Woolfolk, 2004).

Extant research also points to teacher productivity as a key component of a school's impact on student learning (Sass & Harris, 2012). Reasonably, students expect a level of credibility from a teacher. Stephen D. Brookfield, author of a widely used book, *The*

Skillful Teacher, proposed four indicators of teacher credibility: expertise, experience, rationale, and conviction. Brookfield (2006) contended that "students say it is reassuring to know that the person in charge of their learning clearly knows, and can do, a lot" (p. 59). The breadth and wealth of a teacher's expertise are inspiring. Students revere a teacher who not only demonstrates clear mastery of the subject but also can draw on the substantial history of the course. Pedagogical experience enables a teacher to make informed decisions. With respect to rationale, nothing is more reassuring than having a teacher with a well-thought-out plan and a set of reasons informing their actions. Conviction is about making sure that students learn properly the subject matter, the content, or the skills they are being taught. Obviously, these factors are essential to teacher credibility. However, teachers may be deficient in one or two areas but still appear to earn students' trust through hard work and outstanding work ethic.

Several teacher evaluation and accountability tools have been and are currently being used to evaluate teacher performance. Some of the instruments are based or adapted from the following frameworks: North Carolina's *Teacher* Performance *Appraisal* Instrument-Revised, New York State United Teacher's Teacher Evaluation and Development system, Mid-continent Regional Educational Laboratory Evaluation System, Robert Marzano's Causal Teacher Evaluation Framework, Charlotte Danielson's framework, and Kim Marshall's framework. These tools were designed to evaluate teacher instructional leadership, positive learning environment, mastery of content, facilitating learning for students, and reflections on teaching practice.

Operationalizing teacher performance accurately will continue to be a daunting undertaking. No teacher evaluation instrument is perfect. Despite the refinements of teacher performance evaluation instruments over the years, there are always complaints of subjectivity, partiality, favoritism, and observational bias. To overcome these issues, the NEA (2020) proposed a set of principles to guide the design and implementation of a comprehensive teacher evaluation system:

1. Safe and open collaboration is necessary.
2. Measures of teacher performance are most helpful and meaningful when they are based on multiple ratings and clear teaching standards.
3. Integrated systems must link evaluation procedures.
4. Validated evaluation measures are essential.
5. Teachers' input in determining performance and learning outcomes should be part of the evaluation process.
6. Key decisions about assessment and evaluation systems need to be made as close to the local level as possible and in partnership with teachers and their representatives. (p. 7)

The NEA did not foresee a one-size-fits-all solution for all school districts nationwide. It recommended that an effective evaluation system should have three main indicators: Indicators of Teacher Practice, Indicators of Teacher Contribution and Growth, and Indicators of Contribution to Student Learning and Growth. I believe these principles make sense.

Pay-for-Performance Plan vs. Teacher Performance

RAND Education and Labor (2023), a renowned research group on education, reported that most school districts still pay their teachers based on education level and years of service. However, some schools, districts, and states have adopted merit pay systems. Linking teacher pay to teacher performance with the purpose of enhancing student learning has always been problematic within the realm of education because teacher effectiveness is hard to measure. The argument has been that traditional compensation systems offer little incentive for educators to improve student achievement.

Odden and Kelley (2002) examined the efficacy of teacher compensation systems in the United States and found them to be unsuccessful and inefficient as their impact was short-lived. The authors observed that "over a 50-year period, up to about 1995, state and local policymakers enacted several well-publicized efforts to link teacher pay to performance—either their own performance or the performance of students" (Odden & Kelley, 2002, p. 1). Despite this failure, it is rather stunning that many American school districts still consider adopting them as if they were running out of strategies for improving student learning. One can note that these pay-for-performance (PFP) initiatives are not so widespread in American colleges and universities. It is true that anytime there is an educational crisis, solutions are sought from everywhere. Sometimes, it makes sense to recycle and repackage old solutions. If this were the case in 1983 after the release of the National Commission on Excellence in Education report entitled *A Nation in Crisis*, which decried "a rising tide of mediocrity" (Gratz, 2009, pp. 7–8) that threatened the country's schools, its economy, and the nation as a whole, it would have made some sense. Three years later, in 1986, the Carnegie Forum on Education and the Economy released a report on the need to transform teaching into a full-fledged profession (Odden & Kelley, 2002). The two reports called for a revamping of teacher compensation systems.

The 2014 CMS Strategic Plan also considered adopting a performance-based compensation plan as an alternative or supplement to the traditional single salary schedule. It was the centerpiece of the Strategic Plan. The process started in 2007 when CMS, in partnership with the Community Training and Assistance Center, received a Teacher Incentive Fund federal grant for an initiative called

Teacher Incentive Fund–Leadership for Educators' Advanced Performance. By 2011, the initiative was in 20 CMS schools. The benefits of this program are yet to be substantiated. The New York Department of Education and the United Federation of Teachers implemented a similar plan in 2007. It was a 3-year pilot plan that rewarded teachers in high-needs schools who met annual performance targets partly in terms of student growth. RAND Education and Labor (2023) noted the failure of the program. Not only did it not improve student achievement at any grade level, but it also had no impact on teachers' attitudes, perceptions, or behaviors. In other words, the performance bonus program had no motivating effect on teachers, which it was intended to do.

Proponents of PFP regard it as a motivating tactic to attract high-performing and high-quality educators. A PFP system is based on some objective measures of performance, such as student achievement, scores in standardized tests, or demonstrated proficiency in class (Gratz, 2009). The goal is twofold: to improve student achievement and to improve teacher performance. Two foundational premises justify these performance-based compensation schemes: "Higher pay leads to greater motivation [and] greater motivation leads to better results" (Gratz, 2009, p. 20). Thus, the supporting logic is that performance pay increases teacher motivation, which, in turn, increases student academic achievement, as illustrated in Figure 8.

Figure 8. Model of Pay for Performance

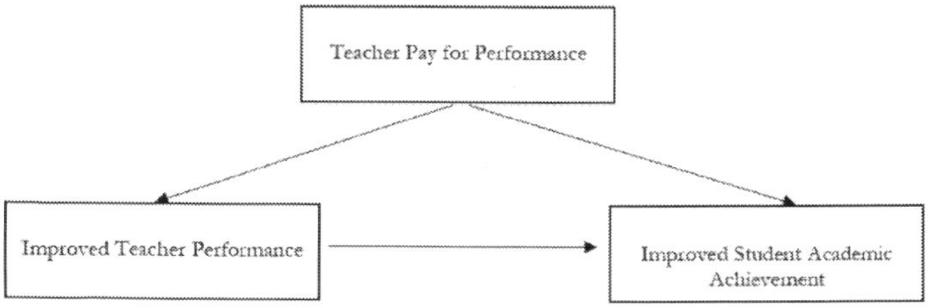

However, these premises are controversial due to the complex nature of teacher performance. The underlying rationale is that linking pay to performance leads to enhanced teacher quality and elevated student performance. It is unclear how performance pay leads to the effectiveness of instructional practice. No known evaluation technique or tool can accurately and credibly quantify and measure teacher performance. It is interesting to note that compensation systems based on merit pay are being adopted by many school districts. More than 20 states and many school districts implemented or considered these pay plans for teachers in 2009 (Gratz, 2009). Naturally, the impact of teaching is elusive, hard to quantify, and rarely immediate. Students may do well on local assessments but fail on state or national standardized tests. Despite the growing interest in PFP programs, they are filled with promises and perils.

The biggest challenge is to have a compensation system in place that considers teacher performance, teachers' credentials, and student outcomes. In other words, teacher pay is aligned with observed teacher performance (Chait & Miller, 2009). While student test scores may be one critical indicator of student performance, no similar construct can measure teacher performance. This raises a question regarding the delineation of actual teacher performance versus perceived teacher performance. Evidently, there is more to teacher performance than student test scores on standardized tests or other learning outputs. Two administrators can observe one teacher concurrently and rate the teacher differently.

Teacher test scores and a preservice teacher's grade point average (GPA) in college are not predictors of effective teaching performance (D'Agostino & Powers, 2009). However, these academic credentials can provide useful data about a teacher's preparation. Other credentials that can provide data regarding a teacher's status include ETS's content-based PRAXIS series test scores, the

National Board Certification Examination, professional licenses, college overall GPA, tenure status, and education attainment.

On a practical level, implementing PFP systems in K–12 education often runs into roadblocks. Measurements of student performance and teacher performance are, at best, imprecise. Several studies have shown the limits of PFP programs. These programs alone do not elevate student achievement. One of the major reasons why these merit-pay systems fail is that teachers' input and insights are never really solicited. Many teachers assume that their feedback does not matter. Once decision-makers have made the decision to pay teachers the way they deem appropriate, nothing teachers can do or say will change their minds. This is the root of the problem. In a study I conducted about CMS teachers' views of the PFP plan, most teachers (89.4%) expressed doubt about the plan for the following reasons: subjective evaluations, implementation problems, unproven plan, lack of collegiality, lack of scientific studies, legality of the plan, parents' accountability, compensation of administrators, teachers' base salary, protection of teachers with many years of experience, and high cost of implementation of the plan. Only 10.6% expressed optimism about the possibility of success of the PFP plan. They thought it could motivate them to improve their performance.

In my survey, I asked teachers whether their pay should be based on their performance. The general consensus among teachers who felt that their pay should be based on their performance was "Yes, but..." They raised some questions about the operationalization of the concepts of "quality" and "performance." Here are a few questions raised: "How do you judge?" "How can quality be measured?" "How do you come up with an agreed-upon definition of quality?" Subjectivity was also mentioned as a potential problem. Overwhelmingly, teachers felt that CMS decision-makers would not consider their input to shape or reshape the PFP plan. It is unclear what their pessimism was based on. It might be useful to probe this question further to learn the source of teachers' pessimism. There was no general consensus among teachers on agreed-upon indicators to measure their performance. Such indicators as content knowledge, engagement, growth, attendance, and parent complaints only provide a partial picture of what a teacher does. Whereas tenure, certification, and education may be easily quantifiable, determining a teacher's salary on the basis of engagement may not be as easy.

Teachers did not agree on indicators of student performance, either. Some of the indicators listed encompassed academic growth, class attendance, behavior, grades, state test scores, common assessments, participation, teacher data, and end-of-course grade or end-of-course exam grade. It could be surmised that teachers were not certain about student performance measures. There was no consensus among teachers concerning the most straightforward way to measure student learning outcomes. Therefore, it is no surprise that PFP architects continue to struggle to find the most effective tools to measure student performance and teacher performance. Failure to operationalize key constructs of student performance and teacher performance may result in terrible calculation errors in teacher salaries. Fundamentally, it is important to treat teacher pay with considerable caution. Teachers often complain about being asked to do too much and receiving too little in return. Before handing a pink slip or a decent check to a teacher, a district must be prepared to provide a plausible explanation about the summation that went into it. Otherwise, the whole pay system may be perceived as arbitrary.

Let's assume that student academic growth is one of the indicators of teacher performance; how is "academic growth" defined? Is it an increase in student GPA over a period of time? Is it an increase in end-of-course or end-of-grade test scores? Is it an increase in SAT scores? Is it an increase in student reasoning? Is it an improvement in students' critical thinking skills? Is it an increase in student awareness of the consequences of academic failure? Or is it an increase in student participation in learning activities? What increase qualifies a teacher for a pink slip? Is it student test scores and student academic growth? Is it student test scores, academic growth, and other variables such as continuing PD, instructional artifacts, evidence of professional growth, and evidence of increased commitment? What academic growth gain will earn a teacher a bonus? Is academic growth measured by quarter, by semester, or by year?

There is more documented evidence of failure than success of these PFP programs. The National Center for Fair and Open Testing (2010) faulted the foundational assumptions they are based on. One of the reasons for the failure is the lack of teachers' support (Lee et al., 2021). Pfeffer (2007) observed that these systems do not always motivate the right behaviors, and the resulting increased differentiation in teacher pay is said to weaken teacher performance. The perception that test scores are the only measure of a decent education limits their functioning as teachers. Teaching to the test is, indeed, detrimental to long-term student learning outcomes (Muralidharan & Sundararaman, 2011). Research has shown that PFP systems can have adverse effects on education, making everyone unhappy. Admittedly, they widen disparities through differential compensation. Basing a teacher salary on the results of multiple-choice questions is indeed unethical and counterproductive, given the complexity of the work a teacher does. The wider the gap between teachers, the less incentive they would have to cooperate and collaborate among themselves, reducing collegiality (Muralidharan & Sundararaman, 2011).

PFP systems can increase teacher stress and anxiety. Another one of their adverse consequences is teacher burnout. It is generally acknowledged that teachers who remain in the profession despite a considerable decrease in their wages may exhibit burnout syndrome behaviors. The term *burnout* is defined as a "syndrome of physical and emotional exhaustion involving the development of negative job attitudes and loss of concern and feeling for others" (Huarng, 2001, p. 15). Conceptually, burnout syndrome has three components: depersonalization, emotional exhaustion, and reduced personal accomplishment. Teacher burnout can lead to absenteeism, tardiness, unpreparedness, and underperformance. This is particularly true for educators whose students display solid content mastery in the classroom but fail to achieve significant academic growth gains in standardized tests for one reason or another.

These merit-based programs impact students in a variety of ways. In the early days of merit pay, British teachers, for example, overemphasized memorization. Responding to pressure to produce results, Gratz (2009) contended that several of these teachers determined that "drill and rote repetition produced the best results" (p. 48). Moreover, the author pointed out that "increasingly, teachers felt 'overpressured' by the system and its enforcers, and they 'overpressured' students to cram to meet the standards" (Gratz, 2009, p. 50). There is ample evidence of these practices in modern American schools with compensation programs tied to teacher performance. It appears that a PFP system may not necessarily be the ultimate solution to improving teacher effectiveness and student learning. This requires a bold support system in place. A successful teacher compensation system needs to be tailored to the unique needs of teachers. Unless the cost of living and other needs of teachers are factored into a decent compensation plan, it would be virtually impossible to get the best out of most teachers. Teaching is bolstered by a strong support system. Teachers should be compensated decently for the hard work they do.

Recommendations

With growing demands for more high-quality teachers due to rising student enrollments, retiring teachers, and chronic teacher attrition, it is commonsensical to make the teaching profession more inviting. This entails improving working conditions and compensation. A compensation system that can restore the profession's lost identity should take into account cost-of-living protection, inflation adjustment, job security, work–life balance, adequate retirement plan, and life insurance policies with living benefits (for example, indexed universal life insurance). I often wonder why teachers cannot have the option of choosing life insurance policies with compound interest and living benefits instead of basic group term life insurance. In short, a good compensation plan should allow teachers not to worry about what Maslow (1970) referred to as physiological and safety needs.

Retaining effective teachers can be astoundingly simple or dauntingly complex, depending on how a school as a whole (leadership, administrators, parents, and students) traditionally treats its teachers. If teachers feel valued, respected, and fairly remunerated, they are likely to recommit. Obviously, compensating teachers equitably is a sine qua noncondition for bolstering the nobility of the teaching craft. In fact, effective school administrators are judged by, among other things, whether they retain effective teachers and how well they cultivate a culture that values teaching and learning (Breaux & Wong, 2003). Unfortunately, there are several reported cases of school administrators blatantly enticing teachers into quitting. I would think a school administrator who has experienced seeing a class without a teacher for an entire semester, as I have, would think twice before encouraging a teacher to quit (unless the teacher is unmistakably awful or harmful to children). Knowing how hard it is to hire and retain effective teachers, what can be gained from such a detrimental, ego-driven decision? I demur.

Other recommended actions to rehabilitate the teaching profession should include reducing the knowing–doing gap through a culture of PD, increasing instructional support, acknowledging the contribution of individual teachers, recognizing the value of diversity, equity, and inclusion, and granting teachers the instructional freedom or autonomy they need to deliver cost-effective, value-added instruction. Subjective evaluations, a skewed view of the leader–teacher relationship, authoritarianism, and a robotic perception of teaching can only drive teachers away from the job they love. Teaching should be less stressful than it is.

The core foundational prism through which teaching is visualized and conceptualized should be reassessed and readjusted. A new framework must consider the breadth, depth, sophistication, and mission of the profession. As much as society entrusts teachers to educate youngsters, it should equally compensate them subsequently, respectfully, and responsibly. To reelevate the status of the teaching profession, society must relearn to consider teachers as real agents of change and transformation, for teaching is a noble profession that births all other professions.

In sum, how a society values education says a lot about its global competitiveness and innovativeness. The United States may lose its dominance if its education system continues to lag behind or decline. Salaries for teachers must be as competitive as for other professions. It is inconceivable that teachers make substantially less money than engineers, computer scientists, bankers, lawyers, accountants, and architects, to name just a few. Yet, without good teachers, there would not be good engineers, good lawyers, good computer scientists, good bankers, and so forth.

References

Adzeh, K. J. (2017). Strategic leadership: An empirical study of factors influencing leaders' strategic thinking. *American Journal of Business and Management, 6*(1), 1–15. https://doi.org/10.11634/216796061706865

Anderson, N. (2009). *Equity and information communication technology (ICT) in education* (Vol. 6). Peter Lang.

Antonakis, J., Avolio, B. J., & Sivasubramaniam, N. (2003). Context and leadership: An examination of the nine-factor full-range leadership theory using the Multifactor Leadership Questionnaire. *The Leadership Quarterly, 14*(3), 261–295. https://doi.org/10.1016/S1048-9843(03)00030-4

Argyris, C. (1982). *Reasoning, Learning and action: Individual and organizational.* Jossey-Bass.

Ashford, E. (2020). *CTE in high school is a bridge to college.* American Association of Community Colleges.

Auguste, E. E., Cruise, K. R., & Jimenez, M. C. (2021). The effects of microaggressions on depression in young adults of color: Investigating the impact of traumatic event exposures and trauma reactions. *Journal of Traumatic Stress, 34*(5), 985–994. https://doi.org/10.1002/jts.22675

Bailie, J. L. (2015). Online graduate instruction: What faculty consider reasonable in relation to what students expect. *MERLOT Journal of Online Learning and Teaching, 11*(1), 42–54. http://jolt.merlot.org/vol11no1/Bailie_0315.pdf

Balsam, K. F., Molina, Y., Beadnell, B., Simoni, J., & Walters, K. (2011). Measuring multiple minority stress: The LGBT People of Color Microaggressions Scale. *Cultural Diversity and Ethnic Minority Psychology, 17*(2), 163–174. https://doi.org/10.1037/a0023244

Banaji, M., & Greenwald, A. (2013). *Blind spot: Hidden biases of good people.* Delacorte Press.

Bandura, A., & Locke, E. A. (2003). Negative self-efficacy and goal effects revisited. *Journal of Applied Psychology, 88*(1), 87–99. https://doi.org/10.1037/0021-9010.88.1.87

Barbash, F. (2015, October 28). The war on "microaggressions": Has it created a "victimhood culture" on campuses. *The Washington Post.* https://www.washingtonpost.com/news/morning-mix/wp/2015/10/28/the-war-over-words-literally-on-some-american-campuseswhere-asking-where-are-you-from-is-a-microaggression/

Barber, S., Gronholm, P. C., Ahuja, S., Rüsch, N., & Thornicroft, G. (2020). Microaggressions towards people affected by mental health problems: A scoping review. *Epidemiology and Psychiatric Sciences, 29*(82), 1–11. https://doi.org/10.1017/S2045796019000763

Barker, R. A. (2001). The nature of leadership. *Human Relations, 54*(4), 469–494. https://doi.org/10.1177/0018726701544004

Bass, B. M. (1985). *Leadership and performance beyond expectations.* Free Press.

Bass, B. M. (1995). Theory of transformational leadership redux. *The Leadership Quarterly, 6,* 463–478. https://doi.org/10.1016/1048-9843(95)90021-7

Bass, B. M., & Avolio, B. J. (1993). Transformational leadership: A response to critiques. In M. M. Chemers & R. Ayman (Eds.), *Leadership theory and research: Perspectives and directions* (pp. 49–80). Academic Press.

Bass, B. M., Waldman, D. A., Avolio, B. J., & Bebb, M. (1987). Transformational leadership and the falling dominoes effect. *Group and Organizational Studies, 12,* 73–87. https://doi.org/10.1177/105960118701200106

Berk, R. A. (2015). The greatest veneration: Humor as a coping strategy for the challenges of aging. *Social Work in Mental Health, 13*(1), 30–47. https://doi.org/10.1080/15332985.2014.890152

Berk, R. A. (2017a). Microaggressions trilogy: Part 1. Why do microaggressions matter? *Journal of Faculty Development, 31*(1), 63–73. https://www.ronberk.com/articles/2017_micro1.pdf

Berk, R. A. (2017b). Microaggressions trilogy: Part 2. Microaggressions in the academic workplace. *Journal of Faculty Development, 31*(2), 69–83. https://www.ronberk.com/articles/2017_micro2.pdf

Berk, R. A. (2017c). Microaggressions trilogy: Part 3. Microaggressions in the classroom. *Journal of Faculty Development, 31*(3), 95–110. https://www.ronberk.com/articles/2017_micro3.pdf

Berk, R. A., Naumann, P. L., & Appling, S. E. (2004). Beyond student ratings: Peer observation of classroom and clinical teaching. *International Journal of Nursing Education Scholarship, 1*(1), 1–26. https://doi.org/10.2202/1548-923X.1024

Billingsley, B. S. (1993). Teacher retention and attrition in special and general education: A critical review of the literature. *The Journal of Special Education, 27,* 137–174. https://doi.org/10.1177/002246699302700202

Blanton, L. P., Sindelar, P. T., & Correa, V. I. (2006). Models and measures of beginning teacher quality. *The Journal of Special Education, 40*(2), 115–127. https://doi.org/10.1177/00224669060400020201

Bligh, M. C., Pearce, C. L., & Kohles, J. C. (2006). The importance of self- and shared leadership in team based knowledge work: A meso-level model of leadership dynamics. *Journal of Managerial Psychology, 21*(4), 296–318. https://doi.org/10.1108/02683940610663105

Borchgrevink, C. P., & Boster, F. J. (1997). Leader–member exchange development: A hospitality antecedent investigation. *International Journal of Hospitality Management, 16,* 241–259. https://doi.org/10.1016/S0278-4319(97)00013-3

Bottoms, G., & Sharpe, D. (1996). *Teaching for understanding through integration of academic and technical education.* Southern Regional Education Board.

Bovill, C. (2020). Co-creation in learning and teaching: The case for a whole-class approach in higher education. *Higher Education, 79*(6), 1023–1037. https://doi.org/10.1007/s10734-019-00453-w

Bovill, C., Cook-Sather, A., Felten, P., Millard, L., & Moore-Cherry, N. (2016). Addressing potential challenges in co-creating learning and teaching: Overcoming resistance, navigating institutional norms and ensuring inclusivity in student–staff partnerships. *Higher Education, 71,* 195–208. https://doi.org/10.1007/s10734-015-9896-4

Braun, V., & Clarke, V. (2006). Using thematic analysis in psychology. *Qualitative Research in Psychology, 2,* 77–101. https://doi.org/10.1191/1478088706qp063oa

Breaux, A., & Wong, H. (2003). *New teacher induction: How to train, support, and retain new teachers.* Harry K. Wong Publications.

Brookfield, S. (1995). *Becoming a critically reflective teacher.* Jossey-Bass.

Brookfield, S. (2006). *The skillful teacher: On technique, trust, and responsiveness in the classroom.* Jossey-Bass.

Brookfield, S. (2015). So what exactly is critical about critical reflection? In J. Fook, V. Collington, F. Ross, G. Ruch, & L. West (Eds.), *Researching critical reflection and research: Multidisciplinary perspectives* (pp. 11–22). Routledge.

Brown, J. D. (1988). *Understanding research in second language learning: A teacher's guide to statistics and research design.* Cambridge University Press.

Brown, R. (1990). Politeness theory: Exemplar and exemplary. In I. Rock (Ed.), *The legacy of Solomon Asch: Essays in cognition and social psychology* (pp. 23–37). Erlbaum.

Bureau of Labor Statistics. (2023). *Occupational outlook handbook, high school teachers.* https://www.bls.gov/ooh/education-training-and-library/high-school-teachers.htm

Burns, J. M. (1978). *Leadership.* Harper & Row.

Capodilupo, C. M., Nadal, K. L., Corman, L., Hamit, S., Lyons, O., & Weinberg, A. (2010). The manifestation of gender microaggressions. In D. W. Sue (Ed.), *Microaggressions and marginality: Manifestation, dynamics, and impact* (pp. 193–216). Wiley.

Castellano, M., Sundell, K. E., Overman, L. T., Richardson, G. B., & Stone, J. R., III. (2014). *Rigorous tests of student outcomes in CTE programs of study: Final report.* National Research Center for Career and Technical Education, University of Louisville.

Chait, R., & Miller, R. T. (2009). *Paying teachers for results: A summary of research to inform the design of pay-for-performance programs for high-poverty schools.* Center for American Progress.

Charmaz, K. (2006). *Constructing grounded theory: A practical guide through qualitative analysis.* Sage.

Chatman, J. A., & Kennedy, J. A. (2010). Psychological perspectives on leadership. In R. Khurana & N. Nohria (Eds.), *The handbook of leadership theory and practice* (pp. 159–181). Harvard Business Press.

Chickering, A. W. (2006). Every student: Can learn—If.... *About Campus, 11*(2), 9–15. https://doi.org/10.1002/abc.161

Cipriano, C., & Brackett, M. (2020). *Teacher, interrupted: Leaning into social-emotional learning amid the COVID-19 crisis.* EdSurge. https://

www. edsurge. com/news/2020-03-18-teacher-interrupted-leaning-into-social-emotional-learning-amid-the-covid-19-crisis

Cohen, J., McCabe, L., Michelli, N. M., & Pickeral, T. (2009). School climate: Research, policy, practice, and teacher education. *Teachers College Record, 111*(1), 180–213. https://doi.org/10.1177/016146810911100108

Combs, H. C. (2009). The selective fossilization hypothesis, focus on form, and the second language classroom: Future possibilities [Teachers College, Columbia University Working Papers in TESOL & Applied Linguistics]. *The Forum, 9*(2), 70–71. https://doi.org/10.7916/d8-5snk-9g23

Conger, J. (2010). *Handbook of leadership theory and practice: A Harvard Business School Centennial Colloquium.* Harvard Business Press.

Constantine, M. G., & Sue, D. W. (2007). Perceptions of racial microaggressions among Black supervisees in cross-racial dyads. *Journal of Counseling Psychology, 54*(2), 142. https://doi.org/10.1037/0022-0167.54.2.142

Corso, M. J., Bundick, M. J., Quaglia, R. J., & Haywood, D. E. (2013). Where student, teacher, and content meet: Student engagement in the secondary school classroom. *American Secondary Education, 41*(3), 50–61. http://www.jstor.org/stable/43694167

Costello, B., Wachtel, J., & Wachtel, T. (2010). *Restorative circles in schools: Building community and enhancing learning.* International Institute for Restorative Practices.

Costello, B., Wachtel, J., & Wachtel, T. (2019). *The restorative practices handbook: For teachers, disciplinarians and administrators.* International Institute for Restorative Practices.

Creswell, J. W. (2007). *Qualitative inquiry and research design: Choosing among five approaches* (2nd ed.). Sage Publications, Inc.

D'Agostino, J. V., & Powers, S. J. (2009, March). Predicting teacher performance with test scores and grade point average: A meta-analysis. *American Educational Research Journal, 46*(1), 146–182. https://doi.org/10.3102/0002831208323280

Dana, N. F., & Yendol-Hoppey, D. (2019). *The reflective educator's guide to classroom research: Learning to teach and teaching to learn through practitioner inquiry.* Corwin.

Darling-Hammond, L. (2000). Teacher quality and student achievement. *Educational Policy Analysis Archives, 8*(1), Article 1. https://doi.org/10.14507/epaa.v8n1.2000

Day, C., Sammons, P., & Gu, Q. (2008). Combining qualitative and quantitative methodologies in research on teachers' lives, work, and effectiveness: From integration to synergy. *Educational Researcher, 37*(6), 330–342. https://doi.org/10.3102/0013189X08324091

DeConinck, J. B. (2009). The effect of leader–member exchange on turnover among retail buyers. *Journal of Business Research, 62*(11), 1081–1086. https://doi.org/10.1016/j.jbusres.2008.09.011

Desai, V., Conte, A. H., Nguyen, V. T., Shin, P., Sudol, N. T., Hobbs, J., & Qiu, C. (2023). Veiled harm: Impacts of microaggressions on psychological safety and physician burnout. *The Permanente Journal, 27*(2), 169–178. https://doi.org/10.7812/TPP/23.017

Dodge, A. M. (2019). Leveraging microaggressions in the classroom as teachable moments: Engaging in difficult conversations as a starting point for change. *Cultural and Pedagogical Inquiry, 11*(2), 53–66. https://doi.org/10.18733/cpi29484

Du Bois, P. M., & Hutson, J. J. (1997). *Bridging the racial divide: A report on interracial dialogue in America.* Center for Living Democracy.

Dulay, H., Burt, M., & Krashen, S. (1982). *Language two.* Oxford University Press.

Duncan, A. (2014). *Guiding principles: A resource guide for improving school climate and discipline.* http://www2.ed.gov/policy/gen/guid/school-discipline/guiding-principles.pdf

Dunne, E. (2016). Design thinking: A framework for student engagement? A personal view. *Journal of Educational Innovation, Partnership and Change, 2*(1), 1–8. https://doi.org/10.21100/jeipc.v2i1.317

Edmondson, A. C. (1999). Psychological safety and learning behavior in work teams. *Administrative Science Quarterly, 44*(2), 350–383. https://doi.org/10.2307/2666999

Edmondson, A. C. (2018). *The fearless organization: Creating psychological safety in the workplace for learning, innovation, and growth.* John Wiley & Sons.

Felfe, J., Tartler, K., & Liepmann, D. (2004). Advanced research in the field of transformational leadership. *German Journal of Human Resource Research, 18*(3), 262–288. https://doi.org/10.1177/239700220401800302

Finn, J. D., & Zimmer, K. S. (2012). Student engagement: What is it? Why does it matter? In S. L. Christenson, A. L. Reschly, & C. Wylie (Eds.), *Handbook of research on student engagement* (pp. 97–131).

Springer Science + Business Media. https://doi.org/10.1007/978-1-4614-2018-7_5

Freire, P. (1972). *Pedagogy of the oppressed.* (M. Bergman Ramos, Trans.). Herder and Herder. (Original work published 1968)

Furuya, Y., Nooraddini, M. I., Wang, W., & Waslin, M. (2019). *A portrait of foreign-born teachers in the United States.* Institute for Immigration Research. https://www.immigrationresearch.org/system/files/Teacher_Paper.pdf

García, E., & Weiss, E. (2019). *Low relative pay and high incidence of moonlighting play a role in the teacher shortage, particularly in high-poverty schools.* Economic Policy Institute. https://www.epi.org/publication/low-relative-pay-and-high-incidence-of-moonlighting-play-a-role-in-the-teacher-shortage-particularly-in-high-poverty-schools-the-third-report-in-the-perfect-storm-in-the-teacher-labor-marke/

Glaser, B. G., & Strauss, A. L. (1967). *The discovery of grounded theory: Strategies for qualitative research.* Aldine.

Glynn, M. A., & DeJordy, R. (2010). Leadership through an organizational behavior lens: A look at the last half century of research. In R. Khurana & N. Nohria (Eds.), *The handbook of leadership theory and practice* (pp. 119–157). Harvard Business Press.

Goe, L., Bell, C., & Little, O. (2008). *Approaches to evaluating teacher effectiveness: A research synthesis.* National Comprehensive Center for Teacher Quality.

Gonzales, L, Davidoff, K. C., Nadal, K., & Yanos, P. T. (2015). Microaggressions experienced by persons with mental illnesses: An exploratory study. *Psychiatric Rehabilitation Journal, 38*, 234–241. https://doi.org/10.1037/prj0000096

Gottfredson, G. D., & Gottfredson, D. C. (2001). What schools do to prevent problem behavior and promote safe environments. *Journal of Educational and Psychological Consultation, 12*(4), 313–344. https://doi.org/10.1207/S1532768XJEPC1204_02

Government Accountability Office. (2022). *Career and technical education perspectives on program strategies and challenges* (Highlights of GAO-22-104544, a report to congressional committees). https://www.gao.gov/assets/gao-22-104544.pdf

Gratz, D. B. (2009). *The peril and promise of performance pay: Making education compensation work.* Rowman & Littlefield Education.

Greenwald, A. G., McGhee, D. E., & Schwartz, J. L. K. (1998). Measuring individual differences in implicit cognition: The Implicit Association Test. *Journal of Personality and Social Psychology, 74,* 1464–1480. https://doi.org/10.1037/0022-3514.74.6.1464

Greguras, G. J., & Ford, J. M. (2006). An examination of the multidimensionality of supervisor and subordinate perceptions of leader–member exchange. *Journal of Occupational and Organizational Psychology, 79,* 433–465. https://doi.org/10.1348/096317905X53859

Gutiérrez y Muhs, G., Niemann, Y. F., González, C. G., & Harris, A. P. (Eds.). (2012). *Presumed incompetent: The intersections of race and class for women in academia.* University Press of Colorado.

Han, Z.-H. (2013). Forty years later: Updating the fossilization hypothesis. *Language Teaching, 46,* 133–171. https://doi.org/10.1017/S0261444812000511

Hare, D., & Heap, J. L. (2001). *Effective teacher recruitment and retention strategies in the Midwest: Who is making use of them?* North Central Regional Educational Lab. https://files.eric.ed.gov/fulltext/ED477648.pdf

Hargis, M. B., Watt, J. D., & Piotrowski, C. (2011). Developing leaders: Examining the role of transactional and transformational leadership across business contexts. *Organization Development Journal, 29*(3), 51–66. https://www.academia.edu/download/46450205/Leaders.pdf

Hartley, B., & Viney, P. (1982). *Streaming English connections.* Oxford University Press.

Heilman, M. E. (2001). Description and prescription: How gender stereotypes prevent women's ascent up the organizational ladder. *Journal of Social Issues, 57*(4), 657–674.

Heilman, M. E., & Haynes, M. C. (2008). Subjectivity in the appraisal process: A facilitator of gender bias in work settings. In E. Borgida & S. T. Fiske (Eds.), *Beyond common sense: Psychological science in the courtroom* (pp. 127–155). Blackwell Publishing. https://doi.org/10.1111/0022-4537.00234

Henfield, M. S. (2011). Black male adolescents navigating microaggressions in a traditionally White middle school: A qualitative study. *Journal of Multicultural Counseling and Development, 39*(3), 141–155.

Herman, K. C., Hickmon-Rosa, J. E., & Reinke, W. M. (2018). Empirically derived profiles of teacher stress, burnout, self-efficacy, and coping and associated student outcomes. *Journal of Positive Behavior Interventions, 20*(2), 90–100. https://doi.org/10.1177/1098300717732066

Hill, C. E., Thompson, B. J., & Williams, E. N. (1997). A guide to conducting consensual qualitative research. *The Counseling Psychologist, 25*, 517–572. https://doi.org/10.1177/0011000097254001

Hinkin, T. R., & Schriesheim, C. A. (2008). An examination of "nonleadership": From laissez-faire leadership to leader reward omission and punishment omission. *Journal of Applied Psychology, 93*(6), 1234–1248. https://doi.org/10.1037/a0012875

Hirak, R., Peng, A. C., Carmeli, A., & Schaubroeck, J. M. (2012). Linking leader inclusiveness to work unit performance: The importance of psychological safety and learning from failures. *The Leadership Quarterly, 23*(1), 107–117. https://doi.org/10.1016/j.leaqua.2011.11.009

Hitt, M. A., & Ireland, R. D. (2002). The essence of strategic leadership: Managing human and social capital. *Journal of Leadership and Organizational Studies, 9*(1), 3–14. https://doi.org/10.1177/107179190200900101

Hollingsworth, D. W., Cole, A. B., O'Keefe, V. M., Tucker, R. P., Story, C. R., & Wingate, L. R. (2017). Experiencing racial microaggressions influences suicide ideation through perceived burdensomeness in African Americans. *Journal of Counseling Psychology, 64*(1), 104–111. https://doi.org/10.1037/cou0000177

Hope, A., & Timmel, S. (1984). *Training for transformation, revised edition I: A handbook for community workers.* Training for Transformation Institute.

Hornor, G. (2018). Bullying: What the PNP needs to know. *Journal of Pediatric Health Care, 32*(4), 399–408. https://doi.org/10.1016/j.pedhc.2018.02.001

Hoxby, C. M., & Leigh, A. (2004). Pulled away or pushed out? Explaining the decline of teacher aptitude in the United States. *American Economic Review. 94*(2), 236–240. https://doi.org/10.1257/0002828041302073

Huarng, A. S. (2001). Burnout syndrome among information system professionals. *Information Systems Management, 18*(2), 1–6. https://doi.org/10.1201/1078/43195.18.2.20010301/31272.3

Humphreys, J. H., & Einstein, W. O. (2004). Leadership and temperament congruence: Extending the expectancy model of work motivation. *Journal of Leadership & Organizational Studies, 10*(4), 58–79. https://doi.org/10.1177/107179190401000405

Huynh, V. W. (2012). Ethnic microaggressions and the depressive and somatic symptoms of Latino and Asian American adolescents. *Journal of Youth and Adolescence, 41,* 831–846. https://doi.org/10.1007/s10964-012-9756-9

Hynes, G. E. (2008). *Managerial communication: Strategies and applications* (4th ed.). McGraw-Hill.

Ingersoll, R. M. (2001). Teacher turnover and teacher shortages: An organizational analysis. *American Educational Research Journal, 38*(3), 499–534. https://doi.org/10.3102/00028312038003499

Irwin, V., Wang, K., Cui, J., Zhang, J., & Thompson, A. (2021). *Report on indicators of school crime and safety: 2020.* National Center for Education Statistics.

Irwin, V., Wang, K., Tezil, T., Zhang, J., Filbey, A., Jung, J., Bullock Mann, F., Dilig, R., & Parker, S. (2023). *Report on the condition of education 2023* (NCES 2023-144). National Center for Education Statistics.

Jenkins, L. (2003). *Improving student learning: Applying Deming's quality principles in classrooms.* ASQ Quality Press.

Johnson, J. L., Adkins, D., & Chauvin, S. (2020). A review of the quality indicators of rigor in qualitative research. *American Journal of Pharmaceutical Education, 84*(1), Article 7120. https://doi.org/10.5688/ajpe7120

Jones, S. M., & Doolittle, E. J. (2017). Social and emotional learning: Introducing the issue. *The Future of Children, 27*(1), 3–11. http://www.jstor.org/stable/44219018

Judge, T. A., & Piccolo, R. (2004). Transformational and transactional leadership: A meta-analytic test of their relative validity. *Journal of Applied Psychology, 89,* 755–768. https://doi.org/10.1037/0021-9010.89.5.755

Judge, T. A., Piccolo, R. F., & Kosalka, T. (2009). The bright and dark sides of leader traits: A review and theoretical extension of the leader trait paradigm. *The Leadership Quarterly, 20,* 855–875. https://doi.org/10.1016/j.leaqua.2009.09.004

Kaiser, R. B., Hogan, R., & Craig, S. B. (2008). Leadership and the fate of organizations. *American Psychologist, 63*(2), 96–110. https://doi.org/10.1037/0003-066X.63.2.96

Keith, J. S. (2016). The impacts of microaggressions on the performance of multiracial and monoracial college students. *PSU McNair Scholars Online Journal, 10*(1), 1–8. https://doi.org/10.15760/mcnair.2016.6

Keum, B. T., Brady, J. L., Sharma, R., Lu, Y., Kim, Y. H., & Thai, C. J. (2018). Gendered Racial Microaggressions Scale for Asian American Women: Development and initial validation. *Journal of Counseling Psychology, 65*(5), 571–585. https://doi.org/10.1037/cou0000305

Kim, J. Y., & Meister, A. (2023). Microaggressions, interrupted: The experience and effects of gender microaggressions for women in STEM. *Journal of Business Ethics, 185*(3), 513–531. https://doi.org/10.1007/s10551-022-05203-0

Kim, L. (2004). Assessment of an on-line educational administration course. *Educational Leadership and Administration: Teaching and Program Development, 16*, 97–110. https://www.learntechlib.org/p/101857/

Kirk, C. M., Lewis, R. K., Brown, K., Karibo, B., & Park, E. (2016). The power of student empowerment: Measuring classroom predictors and individual indicators. *The Journal of Educational Research, 109*(6), 589–595. https://doi.org/10.1080/00220671.2014.1002880

Koedel, C., Li, J., Springer, M. G., & Tan, L. (2017). The impact of performance ratings on job satisfaction for public school teachers. *American Educational Research Journal, 54*(2), 241–278. https://doi.org/10.3102/0002831216687531

Krashen, S. D. (1982). Principles and practice in second language acquisition. *Learning, 46*(2), 327–369. https://lccn.loc.gov/81013909

Krashen, S. D., & Terrell, T. (1983). *Natural approach*. Pergamon.

Latané, B. (1981). The psychology of social impact. *American Psychologist, 36*(4), 343–356. https://doi.org/10.1037/0003-066X.36.4.343

Latané, B., Williams, K., & Harkins, S. (1979). Many hands make light the work: The causes and consequences of social loafing. *Journal of Personality and Social Psychology, 37*(6), 822–832. https://doi.org/10.1037/0022-3514.37.6.822

Lee, J. (2008). Effects of leadership and leader–member exchange on innovativeness. *Journal of Managerial Psychology, 23*(6), 670–687. https://doi.org/10.1108/02683940810894747

Lee, J., Strong, M., Hamman, D., & Zeng, Y. (2021, August 17). Measuring teacher buy-in for the Texas Pay-for-Performance Program. *Frontiers in Education, 6*, 1–12. https://doi.org/10.3389/feduc.2021.729821

Lewis, J. A., Mendenhall, R., Harwood, S. A., & Browne Huntt, M. (2013). Coping with gendered racial microaggressions among Black women college students. *Journal of African American Studies, 17,* 51–73. https://doi.org/10.1007/s12111-012-9219-0

Louis, K. S., Leithwood, K., Wahlstrom, K. L., & Anderson, S. E. (2010). *Investigating the links to improved student learning.* The Wallace Foundation.

Lowe, K. B., Kroeck, K. G., & Sivasubramaniam, N. (1996). Effectiveness correlates of transformational and transactional leadership: A meta-analytic review of the MLQ literature. *The Leadership Quarterly, 7*(3), 385–425. https://doi.org/10.1016/S1048-9843(96)90027-2

Lunenburg, F. C. (2010). Leader–member exchange theory: Another perspective on the leadership process. *International Journal of Management, 13*(1), 1–5. http://www.nationalforum.com/Electronic JournalVolumes/Lunenburg,FredC.Leader-MemberExchange TheoryIJMBAV132010.pdf

Lynch, T. (1996). *Communication in the language classroom.* Oxford University Press.

Maccoby, M. (1996). Resolving the leadership paradox: The doctor's dialogue. *Research Technology Management, 39,* 57–59. https://doi.org/10.1080/08956308.1996.11671065

Makri, M., & Scandura, T. (2010). Exploring the effects of creative CEO leadership on innovation in high-technology firms. *The Leadership Quarterly, 21*(1), 75–88. https://doi.org/10.1016/j.leaqua.2009.10.006

Marques, J. (2006). Awakened leadership: Ancient practice going hip. *Performance Improvement, 45*(7), 35–39. https://doi.org/10.1002/pfi.2006.4930450708

Marzano, R. J. (2017). *The new art and science of teaching.* Solution Tree and ASCD.

Maslow, A. H. (1970). *Motivation and personality* (2nd ed.). Harper.

McCallion, G., & Feder, J. (2013). *Student bullying: Overview of research, federal initiatives, and legal issues.* https://hdl.handle.net/1813/77790

McLaurin, J., & Al-Amri, M. (2008). Developing an understanding of charismatic and transformational leadership. *Proceedings of the Academy of Organizational Culture, Communications and Conflict, 13*(2), 15–19. https://www.proquest.com/openview/0ffa9056df9b-5f17b7679f8da3d35fcc/1?pq-origsite=gscholar&cbl=38769

Meister, A., Sinclair, A., & Jehn, K. A. (2017). Identities under scrutiny: How women leaders navigate feeling misidentified at work. *The*

Leadership Quarterly, 28(5), 672–690. https://doi.org/10.1016/j.leaqua.2017.01.009

Mercer-Mapstone, L., Dvorakova, L. S., Matthews, K. E., Abbot, S., Cheng, B., Felten, P., Knorr, K., Marquis, E., Shammas, R., & Swaim, K. (2017). A systematic literature review of students as partners in higher education. *International Journal for Students as Partners, 1*(1), 1–23. http://hdl.handle.net/10453/162694

Mertler, C. A. (2021). Action research as teacher inquiry: A viable strategy for resolving problems of practice. *Practical Assessment, Research, and Evaluation, 26*(19), 1–12. https://doi.org/10.7275/22014442

Michaels, T. I., Gallagher, N., Crawford, M., Kanter, J. W., & Williams, M. T. (2018). Racial differences in the appraisal of microaggressions through cultural consensus modeling. *The Behavior Therapist, 41,* 314–321. https://psycnet.apa.org/record/2018-52658-003

Miyazaki, T., Shimizu, T., Komaki, G., Fujita, O., Tsuboi, H., Kobayahi, F., & Kawamura, N. (2003). Development of the overt–covert aggression inventory. *Psychological Reports, 93,* 26–34. https://doi.org/10.2466/pr0.2003.93.1.26

Molero, F., Recio, P., García-Ael, C., Fuster, M. J., & Sanjuán, P. (2013). Measuring dimensions of perceived discrimination in five stigmatized groups. *Social Indicators Research, 114,* 901–914. https://doi.org/10.1007/s11205-012-0179-5

Moody, A. T., & Lewis, J. A. (2019). Gendered racial microaggressions and depressive symptoms among Black women: A moderated mediation model. *Psychology of Women Quarterly, 43*(3), 368–380. https://doi.org/10.1177/0361684319828288

Mueller, A. (2019). *How to identify and overcome the mental blocks that slow your creativity.* Asian Efficiency. http://www.asianefficiency.com/productivity/how-to-identify-and-overcome-the-mental-blocks-that-slow-your-creativity/

Mumford, M. D., Campion, M. A., & Morgeson, F. P. (2007). The leadership skills strataplex: Leadership skill requirements across organizational levels. *The Leadership Quarterly, 18*(2), 154–166. https://doi.org/10.1016/j.leaqua.2007.01.005

Muralidharan, K., & Sundararaman, V. (2011). Teacher performance pay: Experimental evidence from India. *Journal of Political Economy, 119*(1), 39–77. https://doi.org/10.1086/659655

Murray, T. A. (2020). Microaggressions in the classroom. *Journal of Nursing Education, 59*(4), 184–185. https://doi.org/10.3928/01484834-20200323-02

Nadal, K. L. (2011). The Racial and Ethnic Microaggressions Scale (REMS): Construction, reliability, and validity. *Journal of Counseling Psychology, 58*(4), 470–480. https://doi.org/10.1037/a0025193

Nadal, K. L. (2018). *Microaggressions and traumatic stress: Theory, research, and clinical treatment.* American Psychological Association.

Nadal, K. L., Griffin, K. E., Wong, Y., Hamit, S., & Rasmus, M. (2014). The impact of racial microaggressions on mental health: Counseling implications for clients of color. *Journal of Counseling and Development, 92,* 57–66. https://doi.org/10.1002/j.1556-6676.2014.00130.x

Nadal, K. L., King, R., Sissoko, D. G., Floyd, N., & Hines, D. (2021). The legacies of systemic and internalized oppression: Experiences of microaggressions, imposter phenomenon, and stereotype threat on historically marginalized groups. *New Ideas in Psychology, 63,* Article 100895. https://doi.org/10.1016/j.newideapsych.2021.100895

Nathanson, D. L. (1992). *Shame and pride: Affect, sex, and the birth of the self.* W. W Norton.

Nathanson, D. (1997). Affect theory and the compass of shame. In M. Lansky & A. Morrison (Eds.), *The widening scope of shame* (pp. 339–354). Analytic Press.

National Center for Fair and Open Testing. (2010). *Paying teachers for student test scores damages schools and undermines learning.* https://fairtest.org/sites/default/files/Pay%20for%20Test%20Scores%20Fact%20Sheet%20final.pdf

National Education Association. (2020). *Promoting and implementing the National Education Association policy statement on teacher evaluation and accountability: An NEA toolkit.* https://www.nea.org/sites/default/files/2020-07/2011NEA_Teacher_Eval_Toolkit_0.pdf

National Education Association. (2023, April 24). *The state of educator pay in America.* https://www.nea.org/resource-library/educator-pay-and-student-spending-how-does-your-state-rank

Neild, R. C., Boccanfuso, C., & Byrnes, V. (2015). Academic impacts of career and technical schools. *Career and Technical Education Research, 40*(1), 28–47. https://doi.org/10.5328/cter40.1.28

North Carolina Department of Public Instruction. (2023). *Career and technical education.* https://www.dpi.nc.gov/districts-schools/classroom-resources/career-and-technical-education

Odden, A., & Kelley, C. (2002). *Paying teachers for what they know and do: New and smarter compensation strategies to improve schools.* Corwin Press.

Ojuola, J., Mostafa, S., & Mohamed, S. (2020, March 4). *Safety leadership functions using complexity science* [Conference session]. The 10th International Conference on Engineering, Project, and Production Management, Singapore. https://doi.org/10.1007/978-981-15-1910-9_33

Okazaki, S. (2009). Impact of racism on ethnic minority mental health. *Perspectives on Psychological Science, 4,* 103–107. https://doi.org/10.1111/j.1745-6924.2009.01099.x

O'Keefe, V. M., & Wingate, L. R. (2013). The role of hope and optimism in suicide risk for American Indians/Alaska natives. *Suicide and Life-Threatening Behavior, 43,* 621–633. https://doi.org/10.1111/sltb.12044

Palanski, M. E., & Yammarino, F. J. (2009). Integrity and leadership: A multi-level conceptual framework. *The Leadership Quarterly, 20,* 405–420. https://doi.org/10.1016/j.leaqua.2009.03.008

Palloff, R. M., & Pratt, K. (2001). *Lessons from the cyberspace classroom: The realities of online teaching.* Jossey-Bass Inc.

Panayiota, F. (2022). Impact of mental barriers on children's learning behaviour. *International Journal of School and Cognitive Psychology, 9*(5), Article 1000253. https://doi.org/10.35248/2469-9837.22.9.253

Papay, J. P., Bacher-Hicks, A., Page, L. C., & Marinell, W. H. (2017). The challenge of teacher retention in urban schools: Evidence of variation from a cross-site analysis. *Educational Researcher, 46*(8), 434–448. https://doi.org/10.3102/0013189X17735812

Pearce, C. L., & Conger, J. A. (2003). All those years ago: The historical underpinnings of shared leadership. In C. L. Pearce & J. A. Conger (Eds.), *Shared leadership: Reframing the hows and whys of leadership* (pp. 2–18). Sage.

Pfeffer, J. (2007). Human resources from an organizational behavior perspective: Some paradoxes explained. *Journal of Economic Perspectives, 21*(4), 115–134.

Pierce, C. M. (1970). Black psychiatry one year after Miami. *Journal of the National Medical Association, 62,* 461–473. https://www.ncbi.nlm.nih.gov/pmc/articles/PMC2611929/pdf/jnma00514-0103.pdf

Pierce, C. M., Carew, J. V., Pierce-Gonzalez, D., & Wills, D. (1977). An experiment in racism: TV commercials. *Education and Urban Society, 10*(1), 61–87. https://doi.org/10.1177/001312457701000105

Porter, M. E., & Nohria, N. (2010). What is leadership? The CEO's role in large, complex organizations. In N. Nohria & R. Khurana (Eds.), *Handbook of leadership theory and practice* (pp. 433–473). Harvard Business Press.

Prewitt, J., Weil, R., & McClure, A. (2011). Developing leadership in global and multi-cultural organizations. *International Journal of Business and Social Science, 2*(13), 13–20. https://ijbssnet.com/journals/Vol._2_No._13_Special_Issue_July_2011/2.pdf

Printy, S. M., & Marks, H. M. (2003). Shared leadership for teacher and student learning. *Theory Into Practice, 45*(2), 125–132. https://doi.org/10.1207/s15430421tip4502_4

Purvanova, R. K., & Bono, J. E. (2009). Transformational leadership in context: Face-to-face and virtual teams. *The Leadership Quarterly, 20,* 343–357. https://doi.org/10.1016/j.leaqua.2009.03.004

RAND Education and Labor. (2023). *Evaluating the effectiveness of teacher pay-for-performance.* https://www.rand.org/capabilities/solutions/evaluating-the-effectiveness-of-teacher-pay-for-performance.html

Rath, C. (2014). *State of America's schools: The path to winning again in education.* Gallup, Inc. https://nurturingfaith.files.wordpress.com/2014/04/gallup-report-state-of-americas-schools.pdf

Rosenshine, B., & Stevens, R. (1986). Teaching functions. In M. C. Wittrock (Ed.), *Handbook of research on teaching* (3rd ed., pp. 376–391). Merrill-Prentice Hall.

Rosenshine, B., & Stevens, R. (1995). Functions for teaching well-structured tasks. *Journal of Educational Research, 88,* 262–268.

Sadker, M. P., & Sadker, D. M. (2000). *Teachers, schools and society.* McGraw-Hill Companies, Inc.

Santoro, D. A. (2011). Good teaching in difficult times: Demoralization in the pursuit of good work. *American Journal of Education, 118*(1), 1–23. https://doi.org/10.1086/662010

Sass, T., & Harris, D. (2012, March 1). *Skills, productivity and the evaluation of teacher performance* (Andrew Young School of Policy Studies Research Paper Series No. 12-11). https://doi.org/10.2139/ssrn.2020717

Schiff, T. (2001). *Priorities and barriers in high school leadership: A survey of principals.* National Association of Secondary School Principals.

Schneider, S., Beege, M., Nebel, S., Schnaubert, L., & Rey, G. D. (2022). The cognitive–affective–social theory of learning in digital environments (CASTLE). *Educational Psychology Review, 34*(1), 1–38. https://doi.org/10.1007/s10648-021-09626-5

Schriesheim, C. A., Wu, J., & Scandura, T. A. (2009). A meso measure? Examination of the levels of analysis of the Multifactor Leadership Questionnaire (MLQ). *The Leadership Quarterly, 20,* 604–616. https://doi.org/10.1016/j.leaqua.2009.04.005

Scott, T. M., Hirn, R. G., & Alter, P. J. (2014). Teacher instruction as a predictor for student engagement and disruptive behaviors. *Preventing School Failure: Alternative Education for Children and Youth, 58*(4), 193–200. https://doi.org/10.1080/1045988X.2013.787588

Selinker, L. (1972). Interlanguage. *International Review of Applied Linguistics, 10*(2), 209–231. https://doi.org/10.1515/iral.1972.10.1-4.209

Shoemaker, P. J. H., Krupp, S., & Howland, S. (2013). Strategic leadership: The essential skills. *Harvard Business Review, 91*(1), 131–134. https://hbr.org/2013/01/strategic-leadership-the-esssential-skills

Sissoko, D. R., & Nadal, K. L. (2021). Microaggressions toward racial minority immigrants in the United States. In P. Tummala-Narra (Ed.), *Trauma and racial minority immigrants: Turmoil, uncertainty, and resistance* (pp. 85–102). American Psychological Association. https://doi.org/10.1037/0000214-006

Smith, W. A., Allen, W. R., & Danley, L. L. (2007). "Assume the position… you fit the description": Psychosocial experiences and racial battle fatigue among African American male college students. *American Behavioral Scientist, 51*(4), 551–578. https://doi.org/10.1177/0002764207307742

Solórzano, D., Ceja, M., & Yosso, T. (2000). Critical race theory, racial microaggressions, and campus racial climate: The experiences of African American college students. *Journal of Negro Education, 69*(1/2), 60–73. http://www.jstor.org/stable/2696265

Startz, D. (2017). *Immigrant teachers play a critical role in American schools.* Brown Center Chalkboard. https://www.brookings.edu/blog/brown-center-chalkboard/2017/03/16/immigrant-teachers-play-a-critical-role-in-american-schools/

Steinbeck, J. (1952). *East of Eden.* Viking Press.

Stephan, W. G., & Stephan, C. W. (1985). Intergroup anxiety. *Journal of Social Issues, 41,* 157–175. https://doi.org/10.1111/j.1540-4560.1985.tb01134.x

Stevick, E. W. (1976). *Memory, meaning and method.* Newbury House Publishers.

Stevick, E. W. (1990). *Humanism in language teaching: A critical perspective.* Oxford University Press.

Strauss, A., & Corbin, J. (1990). *Basics of qualitative research: Grounded theory procedures and techniques.* Sage Publications, Inc.

Strauss, A., & Corbin, J. (1998). *Basics of qualitative research: Techniques and procedures for developing grounded theory* (2nd ed.). Sage Publications, Inc.

Stronge, J. H. (2018). *Qualities of effective teachers* (3rd ed.). Association for Supervision and Curriculum Development.

Sue, D. W. (2010a). *Microaggressions and marginality: Manifestation, dynamics, and impact.* Wiley.

Sue, D. W. (2010b). *Microaggressions in everyday life: Race, gender, and sexual orientation.* Wiley.

Sue, D. W. (2015). *Race talk and the conspiracy of silence: Understanding and facilitating difficult dialogues on race.* Wiley.

Sue, D. W., Alsaidi, S., Awad, M. N., Glaeser, E., Calle, C. Z., & Mendez, N. (2019). Disarming racial microaggressions: Microintervention strategies for targets, White allies, and bystanders. *American Psychologist, 74*(1), 128–142. https://doi.org/10.1037/amp0000296

Sue, D. W., Capodilupo, C. M., Torino, G. C., & Bucceri, J. M. (2007). Racial microaggressions in everyday life: Implications for clinical practice. *American Psychologist, 62*(4), 271–286. https://doi.org/10.1037/0003-066X.62.4.271

Sue, D. W., Capodilupo, C. M., Torino, G. C., Bucceri, J. M., Holder, A. M. B., Nadal, K. L., & Esquilin, M. (2007). Racial microaggressions in everyday life: Implications for clinical practice. *American Psychologist, 62,* 271–286. https://doi.org/10.1037/0003-066x.62.4.271

Sue, D. W., Rivera, D. P., Watkins, N. L., Kim, R. H., Kim, S., & Williams, C. D. (2011). Racial dialogues: Challenges faculty of color face in the classroom. *Cultural Diversity and Ethnic Minority Psychology, 17*(3), 331–340. https://doi.org/10.1037/a0024190

Sutcher, L., Darling-Hammond, L., & Carver-Thomas, D. (2016). *A coming crisis in teaching? Teacher supply, demand, and shortages in the US.* Learning Policy Institute. https://edworkingpapers.com/sites/default/files/A_Coming_Crisis_in_Teaching_REPORT.pdf

Sutcher, L., Darling-Hammond, L., & Carver-Thomas, D. (2019). Understanding teacher shortages: An analysis of teacher supply and demand in the United States. *Education Policy Analysis Archives, 27*(35), 1–36. https://doi.org/10.14507/epaa.27.3696

Swearer, S., & Hymel, S. (2015). Bullying and discrimination in schools: Exploring variations across student subgroups. *School Psychology Review, 44*(4), 504–509. https://doi.org/10.17105/15-0133.1

Tannen, D. (1986). *That's not what I meant!: How conversational style makes or breaks relationships.* Ballantine.

Tannen, D. (1998). *The argument culture: Moving from debate to dialogue.* Random House.

Tepper, B. J. (2000). Consequences of abusive supervision. *Academy of Management Journal, 43,* 178–190. https://doi.org/10.2307/1556375

Thomas, J., & Harden, A. (2008). Methods for the thematic synthesis of qualitative research in systematic reviews. *BMC Medical Research Methodology, 8,* 1–10. https://doi.org/10.1186/1471-2288-8-45

Thomas, J., & Nair, M. (2023). Investigating teacher influence on student engagement in high schools. *The Australian Educational Researcher, 50*(3), 661–681. https://doi.org/10.1007/s13384-022-00511-w

Torres, L., Driscoll, M. W., & Burrow, A. L. (2010). Racial microaggressions and psychological functioning among highly achieving African-Americans: A mixed-methods approach. *Journal of Social and Clinical Psychology, 29*(10), 1074–1099. https://doi.org/10.1521/jscp.2010.29.10.1074

Torres-Harding, S. R., Andrade, A. L., Jr., & Romero Diaz, C. E. (2012). The Racial Microaggressions Scale (RMAS): A new scale to measure experiences of racial microaggressions in people of color. *Cultural Diversity and Ethnic Minority Psychology, 18*(2), 153–164. https://doi.org/10.1037/a0027658

Uhl-Bien, M. (2006). Relational leadership theory: Exploring the social processes of leadership and organizing, *The Leadership Quarterly, 17,* 654–676. https://doi.org/10.1016/j.leaqua.2006.10.007

U.S. Department of Education. (2019). *Bridging the skills gap: Career and technical education in high school.* https://www2.ed.gov/datastory/cte/index.html

U.S. Department of Justice. (2019). *Federal Bureau of Investigation 2019 hate crime statistics.* https://ucr.fbi.gov/hate-crime/2019

Van Vugt, M., Hogan, R., & Kaiser, R. B. (2008). Leadership, followership, and evolution: Some lessons from the past. *American Psychologist, 63,* 182–196. https://doi.org/10.1037/0003-066X.63.3.182

Varkey Foundation. (2018). *Global Teacher Status Index 2018.* https://www.varkeyfoundation.org/what-we-do/policy-research

Vincent, C. G., Inglish, J., Girvan, E. J., Sprague, J. R., & McCabe, T. M. (2016). School-wide positive and restorative discipline (SWPRD): Integrating school-wide positive behavior interventions and supports and restorative discipline. In R. Skiba, K. Mediratta, & M. Rausch (Eds.), *Inequality in school discipline* (pp. 115–134). Palgrave Macmillan. https://doi.org/10.1057/978-1-137-51257-4_7

Vincent, P., & Grove, D. (2012). *Relationships + Rules + Routines = Results: A common sense approach.* Character Development Group.

Vincent, P., & Grove, D. (2013). *Relationships + Rules + Routines = Results: A common sense approach* (2nd ed.). Character Development Group.

Vroom, V. H., & Yetton, P. W. (1973). *Leadership and decision making.* University of Pittsburgh Press.

Walumbwa, F. O., Mayer, D. M., Wang, P., Wang, H., Workman, K., & Christensen, A. L. (2010). Linking ethical leadership to employee performance: The roles of leader–member exchange, self-efficacy, and organizational identification. *Organizational Behavior and Human Decision Processes, 115*(2), 204–213. https://doi.org/10.1016/j.obhdp.2010.11.002

Wasserman, N., Anand, B., & Nohria, N. (2010). When does leadership matter? A contingent opportunities view of CEO leadership. In N. Nohria & R. Khurana (Eds.), *Handbook of leadership theory and practice: An HBS Centennial Colloquium on advancing leadership* (pp. 27–63). Harvard Business Press.

Watson, D., Clark, L. A., & Tellegen, A. (1988). Development and validation of brief measures of positive and negative affect: The PANAS scales. *Journal of Personality and Social Psychology, 54*(6), 1063–1070. https://doi.org/10.1037/0022-3514.54.6.1063

Wei, X. (2008). Implication of IL fossilization in second language acquisition. *English Language Teaching Journal, 1*(1), 127–131. https://files.eric.ed.gov/fulltext/EJ1082599.pdf

Williams, M. T. (2020). *Managing microaggressions: Addressing everyday racism in therapeutic spaces*. Oxford University Press.

Williams, M. T., Kanter, J. W., Peña, A., Ching, T. H. W., & Oshin, L. (2020). Reducing microaggressions and promoting interracial connection: The Racial Harmony Workshop. *Journal of Contextual Behavioral Science, 16*, 153–161. https://doi.org/10.1016/j.jcbs.2020.04.008

Wong, G., Derthick, A. O., David, E. J., Saw, A., & Okazaki, S. (2014). The what, the why, and the how: A review of racial microaggressions research in psychology. *Race and Social Problems, 6*(2), 181–200. https://doi.org/10.1007/s12552-013-9107-9

Woolfolk, A. (2004). *Educational psychology* (9th ed.). Allyn & Bacon.

Wright, A. J., & Wegner, R. T. (2012). Homonegative microaggressions and their impact on LGB individuals: A measure validity study. *Journal of LGBT Issues in Counseling, 6*(1), 34–54. https://doi.org/10.1080/15538605.2012.648578

Yang, Y., & Carroll, D. W. (2016, April 12). *Gendered Microaggression Inventory: Construction and initial validation* [Paper presentation]. Annual Meeting for the American Educational Research Association, Washington, DC, United States.

Yosso, T., Smith, W., Ceja, M., & Solórzano, D. (2009). Critical race theory, racial microaggressions, and campus racial climate for Latina/o undergraduates. *Harvard Educational Review, 79*(4), 659–691. https://doi.org/10.17763/haer.79.4.m6867014157m707l

Zhou, E. (2020). The "too-much-of-a-good-thing" effect of job autonomy and its explanation mechanism. *Psychology, 11*(2), 299–313. https://doi.org/10.4236/psych.2020.112019

Appendix A

Survey for Teachers

Author: Sylvester Ngoma, PhD

Survey for Teachers

General Information

Instructions- Please, check the box that most appropriately applies to you for each item. When you finish, go to the next section.

1. Your school: ______________________________

2. Your age group:

   ☐ 20–29
   ☐ 30–39
   ☐ 30–39
   ☐ 40–49
   ☐ 50 and older

3. Your education level:

   ☐ Some college
   ☐ Associate
   ☐ Undergraduate
   ☐ Graduate
   ☐ Doctorate/ Postgraduate

4. Your gender:
   - ☐ Male
   - ☐ Female
5. Your employment status:
   - a. Full-time
   - b. Part-time
   - c. Other (Please specify):___________
6. How many years have you been teaching CTE?
   - ☐ 0 – 5
   - ☐ 6 – 11
   - ☐ 12 – 17
   - ☐ 18 – 23
   - ☐ 24 – 29
   - ☐ 30 or more
7. What grade level do you currently teach?
   - a. Elementary
   - b. Middle School
   - c. High School
   - d. Other (Specify)
8. What CTE courses have you taught or are you currently teaching?
   - a. ☐ Agricultural Education
   - b. ☐ Business, Finance, and Information Technology Education
   - c. ☐ Technology Engineering and Design Education
   - d. ☐ Trade and Industrial Education
   - e. ☐ Other

9. Number of CTE students (including past years):
   a. 1 – 19
   b. 20 - 39
   c. 40 – 59
   d. 60 – 79
   e. 80 or more.

10. Including the current year, how many years have you taught a CTE course or CTE courses at your school?
    - O 1 year
    - O 2 to 5 years
    - O 6 to 10 years
    - O 11 to 15 years
    - O 16 or more years

11. Including the current year, how many years have you in your district?
    - O 1 year
    - O 2 to 5 years
    - O 6 to 10 years
    - O 11 to 15 years
    - O 16 or more years

12. If you have taught in multiple districts, including the current year, how many total years have you taught a CTE course or CTE courses?
    - O 1 year
    - O 2 to 5 years
    - O 6 to 10 years
    - O 11 to 15 years
    - O 16 or more years

13. Your current teaching assignment grade level (select the answer that best describes your current position):
    - O Grades 6 through 8
    - O Grades 9 through 12
    - O Grades 6 through 12

14. What was your college major? ______________________

15. Your ethnicity:
    a. Asian
    b. African American
    c. Hispanic
    d. White
    e. Native American
    f. Other

Section 1: Perception of Scientific and/Technical Competence

The first section of this survey asks you specifically about others' (including students and colleagues) perception of your competence. Please keep in mind your most recent experience as you respond to the following questions.

How would your students or your colleagues describe your CTE content competence?

____

____

____

____

____

Has anyone (a student or a colleague/an administrator) ever prejudged your ability to perform a task in a CTE class? If yes, can you be specific? What happened?

____

____

____

____

____

Has anyone ever underestimated or overestimated your technical capabilities, your intelligence, or your competence? Please explain. How did you handle it and how did it affect your confidence?

____

____

____

____

____

On a scale of 1 to 10, how confident would you describe your personal ability? ______________________________ Please explain.

Section 2: Perception of Performance

The second section of this survey asks you specifically about how others perceive your performance in CTE classes. Please keep in mind your most recent experience as you respond to the following questions.

On a scale of 1 to 10, how confident would you describe your performance in a CTE class?

_______ Please explain. ____________________________________

____

____

____

____

Has anyone (a student/a colleague/an administrator) ever devalued, invalidated, or diminished your performance or your contribution in a CTE class? If yes, can you be specific? What happened? How did you respond?

____

____

____

____

____

Has anyone ever underestimated or underrated your performance or knowledge in a CTE class? Please provide details.

____

____

____

____

____

How do students or colleagues (or administrators) perceive your expertise, your technical skills and your teaching effectiveness in a CTE classroom? Please explain.

Please describe a situation when your performance was prejudged or rated based on your ethnicity, religion, or gender. What happened?

On a scale of 1 to 10, how confident are you to participate in a discussion or to volunteer to answer questions or to lead a session in a CTE PLC meeting? Please explain.

Section 3: Race and Gender Stereotyping

The third section of this survey asks you specifically about how others perceive your performance in CTE classes based on your race, your gender or your religion. Please keep in mind your most recent experience as you respond to the following questions.

Has anyone ever presumed you to be pedagogically skillful, competent, or incompetent in a CTE class because of your race, your ethnicity, or your gender? Please explain.

Has anyone (a teacher or a classmate) ever devalued, invalidated, dismissed or diminished your performance in a class activity because of your race or your gender? If yes, can you be specific? What happened?

Has a student ever complained to you that he or she felt that you once dismissed, diminished, or devalued his or her contribution or creativity in a CTE class? If yes, can you explain?

____

____

____

____

____

Have you ever received feedback from a student indicating that he or she was hurt by your actions, your words, or your behavior? If yes, please explain.

____

____

____

____

____

Has anyone ever presumed you to be dangerous, creepy, harmful or deviant in a CTE class based on your looks, your race or your gender? Please explain.

____

____

____

____

____

Has anyone ever made implicitly or explicitly biased statements about you in CTE class based on your race, your ethnicity, or your gender? Please explain. How did that statement or those statements affect you?

____

____

____

____

____

Section 4: Cultural Values and Communication Styles

The fourth section of this survey asks you specifically about how others perceive your cultural values and communication styles in a CTE class. Please keep in mind your most recent experience as you respond to the following questions.

Has anyone ever dismissed or degraded your cultural values or your communication style? Please explain.

____

____

____

____

____

Has anyone ever dismissed or degraded your cultural values or your communication style? Please explain.

Describe a situation when you felt that someone dismissed or degraded your cultural values or your communication style in a CTE classroom.

Has anyone (a student, a colleague or an administrator) ever made sarcastic remarks in the guise of humor to degrade your cultural values, your religion, your ethnicity, your gender, your disability, your age, or your sexual orientation? If yes, can you be specific? What happened? How did you respond?

Has anyone in a CTE class ever perceived your communication style or your cultural values as abnormal based on your race, your ethnicity, or your gender? Please explain.

Appendix B

Survey for Students

Author: Sylvester Ngoma, PhD

Survey for Students

General Information

Instructions- Please, check the box that most appropriately applies to you for each item. When you finish, go to the next section.

1. Your school: ______________________________

2. Your age:
   - ☐ 14
   - ☐ 15
   - ☐ 16
   - ☐ 17
   - ☐ 18 or older

3. Your grade level:
   - ☐ 9th grade
   - ☐ 10th grade
   - ☐ 11th grade
   - ☐ 12th grade
   - ☐ Other

4. Your gender:
   - ☐ Male
   - ☐ Female

5. How many years have you been taking CTE courses?
   - ☐ 1
   - ☐ 2
   - ☐ 3
   - ☐ 4
   - ☐ 5

6. What CTE courses have you taken or are you currently taking?
   - a. ☐ Agricultural Education
   - b. ☐ Business, Finance, and Information Technology Education
   - c. ☐ Technology Engineering and Design Education
   - d. ☐ Trade and Industrial Education
   - e. ☐ Other (Specify)

7. How many CTE courses have you taken (including past years) at your school?
   - a. 1
   - b. 2
   - c. 3
   - d. 4
   - e. 5 or more.

8. Including the current year, how many CTE courses have you taken in your school district?
   - a. 1
   - b. 2
   - c. 3
   - d. 4
   - e. 5 or more years

9. Your ethnicity:
   a. Asian
   b. African American
   c. Hispanic
   d. White
   e. Native American
   f. Other

Section 1: Perception of Personal Ability

The first section of this survey asks you specifically about others' perception of your ability. Please keep in mind your most recent experience as you respond to the following questions.

1. How would your teacher or your classmates describe your personal ability?

   ____
   ____
   ____
   ____
   ____

2. Has anyone (a teacher or a classmate) ever prejudged your ability to perform a task in a CTE class? If yes, can you be specific? What happened?

   ____
   ____
   ____
   ____
   ____

3. Has anyone ever underestimated or overestimated your personal capabilities, your intelligence, or your competence? Please explain.

4. How did you handle it?

5. How did it affect your confidence?

6. On a scale of 1 to 10, how confident would you describe your personal ability? Explain your choice.

____

____

____

____

____

Section 2: Perception of Personal Contribution

The second section of this survey asks you specifically about how others perceive your contribution in CTE classes. Please keep in mind your most recent experience as you respond to the following questions.

1. On a scale of 1 to 10, how confident are you to participate in a class discussion or to volunteer to answer questions in a CTE class? Please explain.

____

____

____

____

____

2. Has anyone (a teacher or a classmate) ever devalued, invalidated, or diminished your contribution in a class activity? If yes, can you be specific? What happened?

____

____

____

____

____

3. Is your contribution to class activities as valued as that of other students? If not, explain.

____

____

____

____

____

4. Has anyone ever underestimated or overestimated your personal contribution in a CTE class? Please explain.

____

____

____

____

____

5. How did you handle it?

____

____

____

____

____

6. How did it affect your confidence?

____

____

____

____

____

7. On a scale of 1 to 10, how confidently would you describe your personal contributions? Explain your choice.

____

____

____

____

____

Section 3: Race and Gender Stereotyping

The third section of this survey asks you specifically about how others perceive your performance in CTE classes based on your race. Please keep in mind your most recent experience as you respond to the following questions.

1. Has anyone ever presumed you to be intelligent, academically gifted, or incompetent in a CTE class because of your race, your ethnicity, or your gender? Please explain.

2. Has anyone (a teacher or a classmate) ever devalued, invalidated, or diminished your contribution in a class activity because of your race or your gender? If yes, can you be specific? What happened?

3. Has anyone ever discriminated against you because of your race, your ethnicity, or your gender? Please explain.

4. Has anyone ever presumed you to be a dangerous, criminal, or deviant in a CTE class based on your race, your ethnicity, or your gender? Please explain. What happened?

____

____

____

____

____

5. How did you handle it?

____

____

____

____

____

6. Has anyone ever made biased statements about you in CTE class based on your race, your ethnicity, or your gender? Please explain.

____

____

____

____

____

7. How did that statement or those statements affect you?

____

____

____

____

____

Section 4: Cultural Values and Communication Styles

The fourth section of this survey asks you specifically about how others perceive your cultural values and communication styles in a CTE class. Please keep in mind your most recent experience as you respond to the following questions.

1. Has anyone ever dismissed or degraded your cultural values or your communication style? Please explain.

____

____

____

____

____

2. Has anyone (a teacher or a classmate) ever made sarcastic remarks in the guise of humor to degrade your cultural values, your religion, your ethnicity, your gender, your disability, your age, or your race? If yes, can you be specific? What happened?

____

____

____

____

____

3. Has anyone in a CTE class ever indicated that your cultural values or your communication styles are abnormal? Please explain.

____

____

____

____

____

4. Has anyone in your CTE class ever perceived your communication style as abnormal based on your race, your ethnicity, or your gender? Please explain.

____

____

____

____

____

5. How did you handle each of these occurrences?

6. Has anyone ever made biased statements about you in CTE class based on your race, your ethnicity, or your gender? Please explain.

7. How did that statement or those statements affect you?

8. Have you ever been forced to leave your cultural heritage or cultural values outside in a CTE class? Yes_____ No__________. If yes, can you describe what happened?

____

____

____

____

____

About The Author

Sylvester Ngoma, PhD, is an educator, researcher, and information technology expert based in North Carolina in the United States. Over 3 decades, he has had opportunities to teach, mentor, and coach students and teachers in the United States and overseas. In the United States, his teaching experience includes working as an adjunct professor at College of Information Systems of Trident University International in Cypress, California, a CTE teacher-leader (Expanded Impact Teacher II) at Harding University High School in Charlotte, North Carolina; Web Design instructor at a private high school in Vermont and at the Summer Scholars Program at University of North Carolina at Charlotte (UNCC), and a French instructor at the School for International Training (SIT) in Vermont. Moreover, he served as a director of a youth program in Brattleboro, Vermont. He holds a doctorate degree (PhD) in Information Technology and a Master of Science (MS) degree in Internet Strategy Management (ISM).

His main research interests are (a) microaggressions in career and technical education and in higher education institutions; (b) knowledge transfer, virtual collaboration, and e-collaboration technologies' influences on virtual teams; and (c) information and communication technologies' impact on education. He has authored a number of articles, including "Knowledge Transfer and Team Performance in Distributed Organizations," published by the *Interna-*

tional Journal of Knowledge-Based Organizations. Throughout his years as an educator, he has been intrigued by various aspects of microaggressions in education, social networking groups, and in the workplace in general.

His teaching licenses include (a) Business and Information Technology Education, (b) Technology Education: Scientific and Technical Visualization Endorsement, (c) Technology Engineering and Design Education, (d) Specialized Vocational Education, and (e) English as a Second Language. Dr. Sylvester Ngoma is also a licensed life insurance agent in North Carolina and Maryland. He served as a reviewer for the *International Journal of Sociotechnology* and Knowledge Development (*IJSKD*).

Made in the USA
Columbia, SC
21 August 2024

40402509R00130